PSYCHIATRIC MEDICATIONS
FOR OLDER ADULTS

PSYCHIATRIC MEDICATIONS FOR OLDER ADULTS

The Concise Guide

Carl Salzman

THE GUILFORD PRESS
New York   London

© 2001 The Guilford Press
A Division of Guilford Publications, Inc.
72 Spring Street, New York, NY 10012
www.guilford.com

Printed in the United States of America

This book is printed on acid-free paper.

Last digit is print number: 9   8   7   6   5   4   3   2   1

Library of Congress Cataloging-in-Publication Data

Salzman, Carl.
    Psychiatric medications for older adults: the concise guide /
by Carl Salzman.
        p. ; cm.
    Includes bibiliographical references and index.
    ISBN 1-57230-578-9 (hard)
    1. Geriatric psychopharmacology.   2. Psychotropic drugs.
3. Aged—Drug use.   4. Mental illness—Chemotherapy.   I. Title.
    [DNLM: 1. Mental Disorders—drug therapy—Aged.   2. Psychotropic
Drugs—therapeutic use—Aged.   WT 150 S186p 2001]
    RC451.4.A5 S25 2001
    618.97′68918—dc21

                                                    00-061709

I wish to dedicate this volume to my family members who, as they grew older, taught me how to grow old gracefully. I also dedicate this volume to my patients, young and old, who taught me wisdom and perspective beyond the practice of clinical psychiatry.

ABOUT THE AUTHOR

Carl Salzman, MD, attended Union College in Schenectady, New York, and the State University of New York School of Medicine, Upstate Medical Center, in Syracuse. After an internship at St. Luke's Hospital in New York City, he was a psychiatric resident at the Massachusetts Mental Health Center (MMHC) in Boston, which was, at that time, the major psychiatric teaching hospital of Harvard Medical School. It was there that his interest in psychopharmacology treatment and research began, and following completion of his psychiatric training, he went to the National Institute of Mental Health to work in the Psychopharmacology Extramural Training Program for an additional two years.

Dr. Salzman was then invited to join the faculty at the MMHC and Harvard Medical School, where he has been ever since. As a clinician, he has directed numerous programs at the MMHC, including outpatient clinics and the Day Hospital. In 1979, he became the Director of Psychopharmacology, a post that he currently holds along with Director of Education. His academic advancement led to his appointment as a full Professor of Psychiatry at Harvard Medical School in 1993.

Dr. Salzman's research in psychopharmacology turned toward studying older adults in the early 1970s, when he recognized that virtually no scientific information was available on the use of psychotropic medications to treat older patients. With colleagues at the MMHC, as well as in collaboration with other researchers across the

United States, he began to study the use of psychiatric medications to treat anxiety, depression, Alzheimer's disease, psychosis, and agitation in older adults. In 1984, the first edition of his seminal textbook, *Clinical Geriatric Psychopharmacology,* was published; this widely regarded volume is now in its third edition. More than half of his many published articles, chapters, and reviews have been on geriatric psychopharmacology.

Dr. Salzman has won numerous awards as an outstanding teacher of psychiatry, including sharing the Vestermark Award for Outstanding Contribution to Psychiatric Education awarded by the American Psychiatric Association. In 1997, Dr. Salzman's outstanding research contributions were acknowledged by his receiving the Heinz E. Lehman Research Award for Outstanding Contributions in Research from the State of New York Office of Mental Health. In addition to research, Dr. Salzman maintains an active clinical and consulting practice for patients of all ages. He has also served on numerous national and international advisory committees, including the Food and Drug Administration and the United States Pharmacopoeia. Dr. Salzman has served on the editorial boards of numerous journals, including the *American Journal of Psychiatry,* and has chaired several national task forces on psychiatric research and training including the American Psychiatric Association Task Force on Benzodiazepines: Dependence, Toxicity, and Abuse.

PREFACE

In 1984, when the first edition of my textbook, *Clinical Geriatric Psychopharmacology*, was published, geriatric psychopharmacology, as a specialty of psychiatry, was in its infancy. Very few doctors knew how to prescribe psychiatric medications to older patients, and there was almost no research into the effects of psychiatric medications in older people. Existing textbooks of psychopharmacology typically mentioned treatment of the elderly as an afterthought and advised clinicians simply to use lower doses of medication.

A small group of dedicated researchers scattered throughout the United States recognized this lack of information and began to research drug treatment of the elderly. Among these researchers, my colleagues and I conducted studies on the effects of psychiatric medications in older individuals. Often asked to lecture to practicing clinicians who did not have guidelines for selection of medication, starting doses, or typical daily dose ranges for older patients, I began to appreciate the complexity of arriving at the correct psychiatric diagnosis and drug treatment program for elderly patients. Complications of the aging process, increased likelihood of a concurrent physical illness, and the effects of multiple medications each increase the diagnostic and therapeutic challenge. The need for a book on the scientific basis of drug treatment and the clinical use of psychotropic medications in geriatric psychopharmacology became increasingly apparent.

During this time period, my own parents were aging and approaching death. My personal experiences in coping with their health problems and the side effects of their medications, compounded by their clinicians' lack of information, further convinced me to write a book focusing exclusively on geriatric psychopharmacology.

Now, over 15 years later, the field of geriatric psychopharmacology has grown enormously. Many clinicians from all medical disciplines now specialize in treating older patients, and there are even specific certifications in geriatric medicine as well as in psychiatry. Numerous books and journals focusing on the issues and concerns of the elderly are now available, as are books devoted to geriatric psychopharmacology. As a consequence of this rapid expansion of interest and information, the quality of medical care for the elderly has improved, accompanied by a growing awareness of the special pharmacological requirements and drug sensitivities of older people. A greater selection of medications is now available, and more precise prescribing guidelines have been developed.

In 1998, the third edition of *Clinical Geriatric Psychopharmacology* was published. Almost four times larger than the first edition, it covers a greater range of topics more comprehensively and is regarded by some researchers as the basic textbook in this field. Like the first two editions, it was written primarily for psychiatrists. Practicing clinicians who are not psychiatrists or specialists in geriatric psychopharmacology, however, also need to have a readily available source of information regarding the appropriate use of these psychotropic medications, as do older individuals themselves, their families, and caregivers. All too often, I have been called upon to treat older patients who have developed medication side effects or treatment complications that could have been avoided had the pertinent information been easily accessible to them or their caregivers. *Psychiatric Medications for Older Adults* is intended to provide quick answers to prescribing physicians, as well as to make the principles and practices of geriatric psychopharmacology understandable to clinicians, healthcare workers, and others concerned with their well-being.

The book is organized into chapters focusing on the most common problems that confront clinicians: depression, anxiety, sleep problems, failing memory, and agitation.

At the end of the book, several tables list the psychotropic drugs, recommended doses for older patients, and interdrug reactions (interactions that may occur between psychiatric drugs and other medications commonly taken by older people). These tables have been designed to be useful for both medical professionals and laypeople.

Throughout the chapters, I interpose case vignettes to illustrate important principles of drug treatment in the elderly. The cases are drawn from actual patients of mine, or from patients whose stories have been told to me. The identifying information has been altered and, in some cases, aspects of several patients' histories have been combined to produce one vignette. I thank all these patients who have taught me about geriatric psychopharmacology and have made this book possible.

In order to provide a more continuous narrative without interruptions by reference citations, I have deliberately kept the number of references to a minimum. For interested readers, comprehensive clinical and research bibliographies can be found in the third edition of *Clinical Geriatric Psychopharmacology*.

I firmly believe that not all symptoms and problems afflicting elderly people should be treated with medication, nor should drugs be used conveniently to circumvent a more thorough, multifaceted therapeutic approach. But I do believe that psychiatric medications can be enormously helpful when used properly with appropriate patients. It is my hope that this book serves to facilitate this end.

CONTENTS

Chapter 1

BASIC ISSUES IN TREATING OLDER PATIENTS

"Old age" is commonly thought to begin at age 65. This is, of course, an arbitrary age established in the United States by political agreement and created primarily to define a time of retirement from work and eligibility for social security benefits. Past the age of 65, labels such as "elderly," "senior," and "geriatric" become common. These designations have little or nothing to do with the realities or the relativity of the aging process, nor do they specify a particular state of physical decline or functional characteristics that apply to all people over that age. For example, although most people over the age of 65 have gray hair, having gray hair does not necessarily mean that one is over 65 or old. Although many people over 65 have retired, a significant number of people are able to retire in their 50s, while others work into their 70s and 80s.

In reality, there is tremendous variability in how people age. Many people who are much older than 65 feel and behave as if they were at least 20 years younger; similarly, many people who are barely 65 act as if they were decades older. It is clear that as people age, they encompass an enormous range of both physical and emotional experiences.

The 40-year range of old age, extending from age 65 to the limits of life expectancy (about age 105), comprises the same number of years as adulthood (ages 25–65). These 40-year age spans (whether applied to adulthood or old age) are so broad that sweeping generaliza-

1

tions regarding health, physical capability, memory, disease, sexual function, or quality of life cannot be made, and it is therefore incorrect to assume that universal predictions can be made with regard to response to medications. Nevertheless, certain generalizations concerning the population of persons over the age of 65 are valid. Women live longer than men; women over the age of 85 outnumber men five to two. Two-thirds of the older population are Caucasian; one-third are racial ethnic minorities. For the purposes of this book, it is significant that the number of Americans over 65 is increasing, and the fastest-growing segment of the population is the over-90-year-olds. Centenarians are no longer rare.

Although many older people lead vigorous and active lives, chronic disease is a common companion for a high percentage of persons in this age group. Arthritis, high blood pressure, and heart disease are the most prevalent chronic illnesses, occurring in about 80% of people over the age of 65. There are also normal functional declines associated with the aging process, although time of onset of these changes and the rate of their progression vary greatly. Old people see and hear less well, move more slowly, and tire more easily. Forgetfulness is common, and illness becomes increasingly probable.

Research and clinical experience suggest that old age may be further subdivided at approximately age 80. The health status, physical functioning, and response to medication of most people below age 80 (known as the **young-old**) do not differ greatly from those of middle-aged individuals. However, bodily functions in people over 80 (the **old-old**) deteriorate more rapidly and the prevalence of illness increases as life nears its end. For these old-old patients, prescribing principles and treatment guidelines can accordingly be quite different.

MENTAL DISORDERS OF THE ELDERLY

It has been estimated that from 10% to 20% of older people suffer from mental illness. However, the likelihood of experiencing the first episode of a serious disorder such as mania or depression actually declines past the age of 65. Nevertheless, surveys of older people living in the community have clearly shown that nearly one-third (or more) suffer from *symptoms* of various mental disturbances, especially depression, anxiety, and forgetfulness (Lebowitz, Pearson, & Cohen, 1998). Although not serious enough to qualify as illness, these symptoms may interfere with normal functioning and certainly diminish quality of life.

Mental disorders frequently coexist with physical illness in older people. For example, depression is often seen in patients with Parkinson's disease, thyroid diseases, serious bowel disorders, chronic pain, and in those who have suffered from strokes or heart attacks. Depression may actually precede the development of a physical disorder, as is sometimes the case with cancer of the pancreas or with Alzheimer's disease. More commonly, older people who are physically ill and debilitated become depressed and anxious, and moods and levels of anxiety fluctuate depending on the state of their illness.

WHO TREATS THE ELDERLY?

Surveys of family practice patients indicate a very high percentage of older people seeking relief from psychiatric symptomatology. Outside of hospitals or long-term care facilities, approximately one-third of elderly people receive outpatient medical or mental health care from a family physician, and another one-third do not receive any treatment at all. Only the remaining one-third of elderly outpatients ever receive treatment from a mental health professional. As people age and health declines, they may require hospitalization for medical or surgical treatment, and while a number of older people become depressed or anxious in a hospital, virtually all have difficulty sleeping. It is almost routine, therefore, for older people to receive some form of psychiatric medication in a hospital setting, and this treatment is often provided by clinicians who are not psychiatrists.

MENTAL HEALTH IN NURSING HOME RESIDENTS

There are nearly two million nursing home beds in the United States, with a 90% occupancy rate. In statistical terms, only 20% of old people will ever remain in such a facility, although 5% of persons over the age of 65 are housed in a nursing home at any given point in time. Most residents are women over the age of 80, with significant chronic illness, functional disability, and mental impairment. The majority of older people who live in nursing homes have mental disorders, most commonly dementia, depression, agitation, or some combination of these three conditions, and the number of medications they receive on any given day is substantially higher than that of older adults living on their own. Ranging from two to more than a dozen taken together (Salzman & van der Kolk, 1980), these medications may be helpful for some older people, but for others, having to take so many pills at once can be both uncomfortable and distressing.

OVERVIEW OF PSYCHOTROPIC DRUGS

Psychotropic drugs are divided into classes according to their primary therapeutic indication. The most common reasons for prescribing psychiatric medications in old age and the class of medications used for treatment are the following:

- Depression (antidepressants)
- Interrupted, unrefreshing sleep (hypnotics)
- Diminished memory, concentration, word and name recall (cognitive enhancers)
- Anxiety, ruminations, fears, and phobias (anxiolytics)
- Agitation, inability to relax or obtain rest (antipsychotics, mood stabilizers)
- Psychotic thinking, especially delusions of malevolent influence by others (antipsychotics)

Not all older people who suffer from these symptoms or disorders, however, should be treated with medications. Moreover, whenever possible, medications should not be used if there are effective alternative treatments. Some of these nonpharmacological techniques that can be applied alone or in conjunction with medication treatment include the following:

- Traditional psychotherapy from a mental health professional
- Psychotherapy from a pastoral counselor

- Membership in a support group that consists of other old people with similar problems
- Behavioral training therapy techniques to improve mood, decrease anxiety, and cope with impaired memory
- Appropriate, medically approved daily exercise and physical activity
- Active participation in creative activities (painting, writing, music)
- Active participation in educational activities (Life-Long learning courses, Elderhostel)
- Helping to take care of pets
- Community service, volunteer, and political activities

Psychiatric medications can also be prescribed for nonpsychiatric symptoms, examples of which are shown in Table 1.1.

TABLE 1.1. Classes of Psychotropic Medications and Their Multiple Uses

Type of drug	Symptoms
1. Antidepressants	Treatment of depression, insomnia, decreased appetite, anxiety, chronic pain, panic attacks, phobias, insomnia
2. Neuroleptics (antipsychotics)	Psychotic thinking, schizophrenia, bipolar disorders, agitation, insomnia, anxiety, nausea, hiccoughs
3. Anxiolytics	Anxiety, panic, phobias, insomnia, restlessness, transient stressful situations
4. Hypnotics	Trouble falling asleep, awakening in the middle of the night or early morning
5. Cognitive enhancers	Dementia, memory loss, concentration, agitation
6. Mood stabilizers	Mania, depression, agitation, mood swings, anxiety
7. Anticonvulsants	Agitation, anxiety, insomnia

MEDICATION SIDE EFFECTS

Depending on dosage, all psychiatric medications cause side effects, especially in the old-old and persons who are frail. The higher the dosage, the more likely the development and severity of side effects. Nevertheless, when psychiatric medications are carefully prescribed, using the lowest effective doses, therapeutic benefits almost always outweigh side effects.

On occasion, side effects of psychiatric medications can actually be helpful. For example, drowsiness caused by a drug may be very beneficial if the medication is given at bedtime to an older person who has problems sleeping. More typically, however, side effects make older people uncomfortable or even miserable. A number of drugs cause constipation, forgetfulness, or unsteadiness, all normal and common problems of old age, so that an older person who experiences one or more of these side effects may assume that old age is just taking its toll rather than recognizing medications as the cause. Caregivers should encourage their patients to report any *new* symptoms after they start taking psychiatric medications. Simply reducing the dosage often produces welcome relief from side effects.

It is frequently necessary for older patients to take psychiatric medications for a long period of time, sometimes indefinitely. Some medications, if taken over a prolonged period, induce a physical dependence similar to the way a heavy coffee drinker becomes dependent on caffeine. Dependence on therapeutic medications is not an addiction in the usual meaning of the term as applied to drug abuse, but it can result in withdrawal symptoms if the medication is suddenly stopped. As a general prescribing practice, psychiatric medications should be gradually tapered rather than abruptly discontinued.

POLYPHARMACY

In general, old people take more medications than any other age group and tend to take several medications concurrently because of increasing medical illness in old age. Having to take as may as a dozen (or more) medications may introduce the following problems:

- The possibility of missing a dose is increased because of the different dosing schedules of each medication. It is not unusual to see older persons line up their many medications at the breakfast or dinner table. Consider, for example, how confusing it is to take the "pink pills" only at breakfast (before eating), the "blue and white pills" once per day (at noon, after eating), the "green pills" only at bedtime (with no food). Added to all the vitamins, allergy pills, laxatives, stool softeners, pain pills, and antacids that older people commonly take, the different instructions become overwhelming even for older persons who are not already forgetful.

- An increased likelihood of medication side effects which may confuse the diagnostic picture and interfere with a therapeutic outcome.

- In addition to increased side effects, taking many medications over the course of a day increases the chance that one drug will alter the effectiveness of another. Some psychotropic medications interfere with hepatic metabolism, or with the renal excretion of other medications, thereby raising blood levels of the second drug and contributing to side effects or toxicity. For instance, two commonly prescribed medications, Prozac (fluoxetine) and Paxil (paroxetine), from the class of antidepressants known as selective serotonin reuptake inhibitors (SSRIs), strongly inhibit the metabolism of another class of nonpsychotropic drugs, the cardiac antiarrhythmics, raising the blood level to cardiotoxic levels. Another class of nonpsychotropic drugs commonly taken by the elderly, the nonsteroidal antiinflammatories (such as ibuprofen or Motrin), interfere with the renal excretion of lithium, raising lithium levels to potentially toxic levels.

BASIC RULES FOR TAKING PSYCHIATRIC DRUGS

In order to enhance therapeutic effects while decreasing unwanted side effects, the prescribing clinician, family, and caregivers need to work together jointly with the older patient as a team, in search of the right drug and dosage that will improve the patient's health and well-being. The patient's role is to take the medication as prescribed and report the effects as accurately and frequently as is practical. The prescriber's role is to know the pharmacology of the medications, their side effects, and potential drug interactions, as well as the dosage adjustments that are necessary for older people. It is also the prescriber's responsibility to ensure that appropriate medical evaluation and diagnostic tests are performed before psychiatric medication is prescribed. The following medical evaluations are recommended:

1. Obtain accurate information regarding all medications the older person is taking, including hormones, over-the-counter medicines, vitamins, and herbal preparations.
2. Obtain accurate information regarding alcohol, tobacco, or other drug use.
3. Obtain an accurate description of the symptoms. This may require interviewing family, spouse, caregivers, or even friends.
4. Obtain as complete a history of past medical or psychiatric illnesses as possible. Older people may forget their earlier psychiatric history.
5. Conduct a physical examination.
6. Conduct a brief mental status exam.
7. Obtain a complete blood count (CBC) and routine laboratory tests, including differential and urinalysis.
8. Obtain liver function tests, thyroid function tests, and measures of vitamin B_{12} and folic acid levels.
9. An electrocardiogram is helpful, but it is essential if tricyclic antidepressants or beta blockers are to be prescribed.

Spouses or caregivers of older people (typically the frail, the medically ill, or the very old) who need assistance with their medication commonly assume the role of dispensing it, and therefore need to be questioned carefully regarding the patient's current medication status.

GUIDELINES FOR OLDER PATIENTS, CAREGIVERS, AND FAMILY MEMBERS

It is useful for the prescribing clinician to provide the following information in large print and easily understandable language to patients, their families, and caregivers:

- The name of the drug, its purpose, and starting dose.
- Common side effects of the medication.
- Side effects that are especially likely to develop in older people.
- Possible interdrug reactions and any guidelines for mixing (or not mixing) certain medications.
- Instructions to take the medications only as prescribed, not more, not less; not more or less often.
- Most importantly, instructions to stay in close touch with the doctor and report any changes or unusual effects.
- Advice to discontinue smoking and sharply limit alcohol and caffeine use.
- Warnings about excessive alcohol use.
- Warnings about driving when taking psychiatric medications.
- How often office visits or checkups are necessary, and how the prescriber can be reached by telephone in emergencies.
- Treatments other than medications.
- A warning never to discontinue psychiatric medication abruptly unless instructed to do so by the prescriber.

When the correct medications are selected for appropriate patients, and when adequate but not excessive doses are used for designated periods of time, clinicians and patients can expect a reduction of symptoms in most cases. The rate of recovery is highly variable and is usually longer for old people than for younger and middle-aged sufferers. It is possible to treat older patients successfully with only a minimum of attendant problems when adhering to the basic prescribing guidelines shown in Table 1.2 on page 10.

FACILITATING TREATMENT COMPLIANCE IN OLDER PATIENTS

Compliance is the term used to describe taking a medication according to the instructions of the prescribing clinician; noncompliance is the failure to do so. Noncompliance among older people is quite high (Avorn, 1998). The most common causes of noncompliance in the elderly are shown in Table 1.3 on page 11.

Older people usually take fewer medications than prescribed; only

TABLE 1.2. Basic Prescribing Guidelines for Use with Older Patients

1. Take a careful history. Some symptoms are normal responses to problems of late life and not evidence of psychopathology.

2. Conduct a careful medical evaluation to rule out nonpsychiatric causes of the psychiatric disorder.

3. Check for drug side effects or drug interactions as a cause of symptoms.

4. Start medication treatment with low doses. Follow the maxim: "Start low and go slow."

5. Maintain close contact with patient, family, and caregivers.

6. Dosage adjustments may need to be frequent; doses will vary over time as the person continues to age.

7. Stay alert for new additional medications that the older patient may be taking during the course of treatment. New drug interactions and new side effects may develop over time.

occasionally do they take more. Most noncompliance is unintentional, but the high cost of psychiatric medications and the lack of insurance subsidy frequently contribute to noncompliance. It is not unusual for older people to spend a significant portion of their weekly income on medications. Newspapers commonly report tragic stories of older patients being unable to afford life-maintaining medications or having to choose between drugs because of cost. Clinicians and caretakers must be sensitive to this issue and skillfully determine when cost is a possible cause of noncompliance.

In general, clinicians and family members should be aware of an older person's attitude toward medication. Some may not believe in taking any medication, or may believe their symptoms to be either part of getting old or beyond treatment. In such circumstances, a family member or caregiver must assume responsibility for administering the medications. For those elders who are compliant but forgetful, commercially available pillboxes, with day or time of day clearly labeled, can be purchased. Sometimes it is helpful to encourage older

TABLE 1.3. Causes of Medication Noncompliance in the Elderly

- Poor doctor–patient communication
- Inadequately understood instructions
- Forgetfulness
- Inability to read labels of drug containers
- Lifelong wariness or avoidance of medications
- Difficulty opening drug containers
- Many drugs being taken simultaneously
- Side effects
- Lack of insight into illness and the necessity for medication
- Cost of medications

persons to keep a "logbook" in which they record the date and time the medication is taken, and any side effects.

Also, practical problems common in old age can interfere with an older person's ability to take medication according to instructions. The printed label on a pill container may be too small for an older person to read accurately, even with glasses. Pill containers with safety caps can be extremely difficult to open, especially for people with arthritic hands, muscle weakness, or chronic pain. Large pills may be difficult to swallow; liquids may taste terrible.

Habitual behavior can help improve compliance. Labeled pillboxes can be filled the night before, so that they will be readily available the following day. Signs with large print, or even pictures of the pills with their names and purpose, can help a visually impaired person take medications as prescribed. New computerized techniques such as automatic phone call reminders, reminders from pharmacies to renew prescriptions, and even electronic beeper-type pill containers are being developed.

Probably the most common reason that older people stop taking medications as prescribed is the development of one or more side effects (see Table 1.4 on page 12).

Older people are increasingly likely to experience these side effects because of several age-related factors. First, structural and functional changes throughout the body and central nervous system often (but not always) increase sensitivity to psychotropic drug effects, causing toxicity from doses routinely prescribed for younger adults. Sec-

TABLE 1.4. Side Effects That Commonly Cause Medication Noncompliance

• Drowsiness	• Agitation
• Dry mouth	• Forgetfulness
• Constipation	• Blurred vision
• Unsteadiness	

ond, the aging body tends to metabolize and excrete drugs less efficiently, leading to higher levels of unmetabolized drugs in the central nervous system for longer periods. Third, multiple drugs taken by older people increase the risk of drug interactions and side effects. Examples of the common pharmacological properties of psychotropic drugs and the side effects that they produce are shown in Table 1.5.

TABLE 1.5. Common Side Effects of Psychotropic Drugs in Older People

Drug effect	Symptoms
1. Decreased central nervous system arousal level	Sedation, apathy, fatigue, withdrawal, depressed mood, disinhibition, confusion
2. Peripheral anticholinergic blockade	Dry mouth, constipation, atonic bladder, blurry vision
3. Central anticholinergic blockade	Confusion, disorientation, forgetfulness, agitation, assaultiveness, visual hallucinosis
4. Alpha-adrenergic blockade and central pressor blockade	Orthostatic hypotension
5. Dopaminergic blockade	Extrapyramidal symptoms, tardive dyskinesia, agitation

Psychotropic drugs that make older people drowsy during the daytime interfere with their activities of daily living, may make them feel more depressed, and may worsen agitation and insomnia at night. Anticholinergic side effects such as constipation, dry mouth, blurred vision, and trouble urinating—usually an annoyance in younger adults—may be extremely disabling to older individuals who already have some of these problems due to advanced age. Several categories of psychotropic drugs, such as antidepressants and benzodiazepines, cause unsteadiness and have been associated with falls and consequent injuries or fractures. Sedative or anticholinergic psychiatric medications commonly make memory and concentration worse, especially in the older person already experiencing memory difficulties.

Given these side effects, it is not surprising that older people do not always take their medications as prescribed. Furthermore, physicians may not always be informed of noncompliance due to side effects. Some older patients are embarrassed to admit that they are not taking their medications as prescribed; others may not even be aware that they regularly forget to take their pills. Caregivers as well as family members need to be more aware of the older individual who is either not taking the medications or who, less commonly, is taking more than the prescribed amount.

Since multiple medications tend to increase the likelihood of noncompliance, prescribers should endeavor to speak with other prescribing clinicians to determine whether some medications can be eliminated (or dose frequency reduced) so as to simplify the overall drug-taking regimen. In order to reduce noncompliance due to side effects, prescribers and caregivers need to monitor their development carefully. Dosing schedules that can be simplified, or medications that can be changed to relieve side effects, will enhance drug-taking compliance.

Since noncompliance interferes with treatment and prolongs suffering, caregivers, family members, and clinicians must carefully account for the pills. For older people living at home, the spouse usually assumes the role of dispensing the medication. This system works well as long as the spouse is capable of performing this function and the marital relationship is stable and supportive. But some older married couples have been battling for years and, in old age, barely communicate. Should such acrimony exist, it is not surprising if the spouse does not always accurately dispense the medication. Even in the context of a loving relationship, the infirm, frail, or ill spouse may also have difficulties taking and dispensing medications. One can readily imagine a home setting in which two very elderly people are each taking several (or many!) different medications at different times of the day; confusion, forgetfulness, and unintentional noncompliance are almost inevitable. Such problems are avoided in hospitals, assisted-living facilities, and nursing homes, where medication is dispensed by professional caregivers.

Chapter 2

DEPRESSION

Feeling depressed or "down" is quite common in older people but the sadness, sense of loss, and periods of unhappiness that inevitably occur in late life are not necessarily evidence of clinical depression. Developing a diagnosable depression is *not* an inevitable part of aging, and most old people do not suffer from the pervasive and debilitating illness that psychiatrists call "major depressive disorder." Surveys of older people living in the community, however, have indicated that *symptoms* of depression, such as unhappiness, fatigue, and a sense of pointlessness, are quite common. For example, at any given time, approximately one out of every five older individuals has a significant number of depressive symptoms, and at least one in six older patients visiting a primary care physician's office has a significant degree of depression (Katz, Miller, & Oslin, 1998). Depressive symptoms or major depressive disorder occur in more than one out of every ten older patients hospitalized for medical purposes (Williams-Russo, 1996), and one-fourth or more of old people in nursing homes may also suffer from a clinical depression or depressive symptomatology (Rovner & Katz, 1993). Most importantly, the prevalence of significant depressive symptoms increases in old people who have chronic medical disorders and disabilities.

DIAGNOSING DEPRESSION IN OLDER PATIENTS

It is extremely important to determine whether an older person is suffering from a clinical depressive disorder as opposed to the normal fluctuations in mood that typically include "down" days. Depression interferes with an older person's quality of life, which, in many cases, has already become increasingly limited by the natural changes of aging. The following early warning signs that may become obvious to family and friends, and about which clinical caregivers can inquire, signal that a major depression is developing:

- Loss of interest in usual activities
- Decreased social interaction
- More time spent in bed
- Decreased grooming
- Increased irritability

A depressive disorder in elders is usually quite easy to recognize. The older person appears morose and listless, and complains of little appetite, difficulty falling asleep, and frequent awakening. Individuals who have previously been actively involved with family and friends, interested in their own and others' daily lives, now become withdrawn, listless, and apathetic. Some complain bitterly about how unhappy they are, speaking of nothing except their suffering; others seem resigned and behave as if life has nothing more to offer them. Reassurance or attempts to encourage positive thinking are useless.

Clinical depression encompassing a range of moods and disturbed affect is usually divided into three subtypes: major depressive disorder, the most serious form; dysthymic disorder, a chronic but less severe state of depression usually mixed with anxiety; and minor or sub-syndromal depression, in which depressive symptoms are persistent but not severe. The DSM-IV diagnostic criteria for major depressive disorder are shown in Table 2.1 (American Psychiatric Association, 1994). Compared with younger adults, older depressed patients show fewer symptoms of guilt and self-reproach, and more disturbances in patterns of sleep, appetite, and energy level.

Although the diagnosis of major depression is often obvious, diagnostic indicators are sometimes more obscure. Some older people who display significant depressive symptoms and apathy at home are embarrassed to appear depressed in front of a stranger and become ani-

TABLE 2.1. Diagnostic Criteria for Major Depressive Disorder

Five (or more) of the following symptoms have been present during the same 2-week period and represent a change from previous functioning; at least one of the symptoms is either (1) depressed mood or (2) loss of interest or pleasure.

(1) depressed mood most of the day, nearly every day, as indicated by either subjective report (e.g., feels sad or empty) or observation made by others (e.g., appears tearful)

(2) markedly diminished interest or pleasure in all, or almost all, activities most of the day, nearly every day (as indicated by either subjective account or observation made by others)

(3) significant weight loss when not dieting or weight gain (e.g., a change of more than 5% of body weight in a month), or decrease or increase in appetite nearly every day

(4) insomnia or hypersomnia nearly every day

(5) psychomotor agitation or retardation nearly every day (observable by others, not merely subjective feelings of restlessness or being slowed down)

(6) fatigue or loss of energy nearly every day

(7) feelings of worthlessness or excessive or inappropriate guilt (which may be delusional) nearly every day (not merely self-reproach or guilt about being sick)

(8) diminished ability to concentrate, or indecisiveness, nearly every day (either by subjective account or as observed by others)

(9) recurrent thoughts of death (not just fear of dying), recurrent suicidal ideation without a specific plan, or a suicide attempt or a specific plan for committing suicide

Note. From American Psychiatric Association (1994). Copyright 1994 by the American Psychiatric Association. Adapted by permission.

mated and engaging when taken to a doctor. For reasons that are poorly understood, common physical symptoms such as stomach pains, poor digestion, shifting aches and pains in the back, and unpleasant tastes in the mouth may suggest depression in old people. Depressed elders who suffer from such nonspecific physical symptoms often make numerous visits to physicians but do not obtain relief with medications. Nor are they reassured when the physical examinations or medical test procedures prove negative.

The classic signs of sadness, tearfulness, loss of energy, disturbed sleep and appetite, and expressions of hopelessness and futility that usually indicate clinical depression are less reliable signs of depression in the very elderly. Virtually all old people have some difficulties with sleep, commonly awakening very early in the morning. Appetite may be decreased for simple but unrecognized reasons, such as poorly fitting dentures. Diminished physical energy is also quite common in normal old age, and statements such as "I am prepared to die" may actually be a healthy adaptation to realistic circumstances.

Very severe depression is usually obvious, but older people may also suffer milder forms of depression that are more difficult to recognize. Persistent milder forms of depression, termed **dysthymic disorder** or **subsyndromal depression**, may be indistinguishable from signs of illness or appropriate responses to loss of health, loved ones, and functional ability. Furthermore, circumstances that accompany old age, such as moving to an institutional residence or to a new city in order to be closer to children, may precipitate a depression. However, when the depressed mood *dominates* an older person's daily life, treatment is indicated even if there is an appropriate cause for the disturbed mood.

THE CASE OF MR. A: THE SLIDE FROM SADNESS TO CLINICAL DEPRESSION

Mr. A, an 84-year-old gentleman, was obviously in great distress. His eyes were almost continually moist, and he would break into tears when asked almost any question. He often woke during the night following disturbing nightmares, and he had no appetite.

Mr. A was a Holocaust survivor who had lost most of his family in the death camps. His depressive symptoms were characterized by persistent memories of his lost family and the horrors they had all suffered during the war. At first, the physician viewed Mr. A's severe depressive symptoms as the inevitable consequence of his earlier traumatic experiences. Further questioning, however, revealed that Mr. A had not always been depressed. Following the war, he was successful in business and led an active and involved social life, following current events in newspapers in five languages.

Mr. A's current depression, following the pattern of previous episodes that had simply appeared and disappeared, had no apparent cause. During each depressive episode, he would become preoccupied by his Holocaust experience. However, he responded well to antidepressant medication and, when not depressed, these experiences receded into the background and he led a contented and fulfilled life.

The physical appearance of an older person can be misleading in the evaluation of the presence or absence of a depressive disorder. Signs of depression, however, are often visible if one knows where to look. For example, an impeccably dressed older person who is depressed may fidget and not meet the clinician's gaze, or may sigh deeply before responding to each question. One older person with depression may seem more worried than sad and will try to ascribe all symptoms to realistic worries about money or a spouse's health. Another will insist that it is not a matter of depression but "just getting old." When asked about a lack of interest in socializing, exercising, reading, watching television, or other activities that formerly brought pleasure, an older person with depression might respond by finding fault with the activity or simply blaming others. Sweeping generalizations such as "All my friends have died," or "They don't have anything good on television anymore," or "Nobody cares about me anymore," can indicate an underlying clinical depression. While denying feeling depressed, some older people might then launch into a litany of bitter and unrealistic complaints, which should also raise the possibility of an underlying depression.

Table 2.2 on page 20 lists both useful and misleading diagnostic clues that might or might not indicate the presence of a depressive disorder in an old person.

The signs and symptoms of clinical depression further shift in

TABLE 2.2. Diagnostic versus Unreliable Clues to Late-Life Depression

Useful diagnostic clues	Unreliable diagnostic clues
Unusually slow movements	Trouble falling asleep, or early morning awakening
Unusual irritability	Diminished appetite
Withdrawal of interest in usual behaviors	Diminished physical energy
Spontaneous comments about a wish to die in order to end suffering	"I'm prepared to die"
Unusually poor state of grooming	Sighing
Unusually poor state of dress	Tears
Very slow speech	Sad face

persons over the age of 80 (the old–old). It is less common for people over 80 to have the array of symptoms listed in Table 2.1, making depression harder to diagnose. The old–old become more irritable and less socially interactive, and often complain about other people's behavior as a cause for their unhappiness. It is not unusual for very old people with depression to complain bitterly about their nursing home roommates, ungrateful children and family members, and the lack of help or consideration shown them by the staff of an assisted–living facility. Although these complaints may have some basis in reality, they are often exaggerated and may even become an obsessive focus. The case of Mrs. B illustrates the way in which some older people express their depressive symptoms.

THE CASE OF MRS. B: DENYING DEPRESSION

Mrs. B, an 82-year-old woman, had been living in an excellent nursing home for 6 years. She had insisted on selling her home and moving to the nursing home despite cautious warnings from her children. Her physical health was good, without signs of dementia or even failing memory. Mrs. B appeared unhappy to the staff, but she denied feeling bad when directly questioned. Instead, she contended that all her troubles began when she moved to the nursing home. The nurses noted a dejected elderly woman who typically sat alone in the hallway, either not talking with any other residents or complaining. When they attempted to talk to her, she would only lament the loss of her home and her dismay at being a nursing home resident. She sighed periodically and became tearful, and often fidgeted with her dress and her hair. She steadfastly denied feeling depressed.

The doctors observed Mrs. B's lack of interest in the social life of the nursing home. She had virtually no interest in food and was gradually losing weight and becoming increasingly frail. They also noted that her sleep was interrupted more frequently than most of the other residents, and that she had little energy or enthusiasm. When the doctors asked her if she wished that she were dead, she would sigh, roll her eyes, and stare intently at them. "I do not wish to hurt myself," she would say, "but I wish God would take me in the night and I wouldn't wake up in the morning." When asked if she looked forward to anything, she would look exasperated and, after a long pause, answer fiercely, "What is there to look forward to in a place like this?"

These were classic signs and symptoms of late-life depression. When treated with an antidepressant, Mrs. B's complaints gradually disappeared and she became active in the many programs offered by the nursing home.

PROBING FOR SUICIDAL THOUGHTS AND TENDENCIES

Suicide is most common in regions of the United States with the greatest density of older retired people, among whom the risk of suicide is especially high in recently bereaved older men. Prior suicide attempts further increase the risk, as does the suicide of a family member or friend.

Family members and friends are sometimes reluctant to inquire about suicidal thoughts in an older person in the mistaken belief that asking about suicide may plant an idea that was not previously present.

Significantly, the opposite is true. Asking about suicide diminishes the sense of isolation that older people with depression often feel and reduces the risk.

It is imperative that clinicians ask an older person with depression about suicidal thoughts. If suicidal thoughts dominate a person's thinking, or if specific plans have been made, hospitalization is necessary. This is a delicate matter to raise with some older individuals who may view it as a shameful sign of their failure to cope with life's problems. Clinicians should gently but firmly reassure the older person that suicidal thoughts are symptoms of a treatable illness, and that the time spent in hospital is likely to be brief. It is important to emphasize that being hospitalized is not being "put away" permanently.

The following guidelines should be observed when responding to an older person with depression who is preoccupied with suicidal thoughts or has attempted suicide in the past and is currently suicidal:

- The person should not be left alone.
- Hospitalization will be necessary unless the person can be continually monitored for an entire 24-hour period.
- Specific plans for committing suicide constitute a very high risk, but the absence of plans does not necessarily mean there is no immediate risk.
- Any medication that has lethal potential in overdose must be supervised, and potential weapons must be removed.
- The risk of suicide does not decrease as soon as the patient begins taking antidepressant medication. During the early period of antidepressant treatment, the risk of suicide may actually increase.
- Antidepressant medications and doses are the same whether or not a depressed older person is suicidal.

RELATIONSHIP BETWEEN PHYSICAL ILLNESS AND DEPRESSION

It is normal to feel down in the dumps or depressed when sick, especially if illness has been present for a long time. Chronic and disabling disorders such as arthritis, heart disease, or life-threatening cancer are frequently associated with depression in late life. Some illnesses are predictably associated with depression (see Table 2.3).

Neurological disorders in the elderly are particularly associated with depression. For example, poststroke depression may develop in as many as half of all older patients during the acute period and, after 1

TABLE 2.3. Medical Illnesses Associated with Depression

Cardiovascular disease	Infectious disease
Angina pectoris	Hepatitis
*Coronary bypass surgery	HIV infection
*Myocardial infarction	Infectious mononucleosis
Central nervous system disease	*Influenza
*Alzheimer's disease	Lyme disease
Amyotrophic lateral sclerosis	Tertiary syphilis
Huntington's disease	Viral encephalitis
Migraine	Neoplastic and systemic disease
*Multiple sclerosis	*Carcinoma of the pancreas
Myasthenia gravis	Disseminated carcinomatosis
Neoplasms	Liver failure
Paraneoplastic syndromes	Rheumatoid arthritis
*Parkinson's disease	Systemic lupus erythematosus
*Stroke	Temporal arteritis
*Vascular dementia	Uremia
Electrolyte imbalances	Nutritional deficiencies
Hypercalcemia	*Vitamin B_{12} deficiency
Hyperkalemia	*Folic acid deficiency
Hypokalemia	Iron deficiency
Hyponatremia	Protein deficiency
Endocrine disorders	Thiamine deficiency
Addison's disease	
*Autoimmune thyroiditis	
*Cushing's disease	
Diabetes mellitus	
Hyperparathyroidism	
Hyperthyroidism	
*Hypothyroidism	

Note. Illnesses most commonly associated with the elderly are indicated by an asterisk (*).

year, more than 50% of men and 30% of women continue to be depressed (Robinson, Schultz, & Paradiso, 1998). Stroke-related depression is probably due to a combination of factors, including structural changes in specific sites in the brain as well as the psychological impact of having had a stroke. Fortunately, patients with poststroke depression often respond to antidepressant medication. The complicated relationship between having a stroke (even a very mild one) and developing a depression is illustrated by the case of Mr. C.

THE CASE OF MR. C: POSTSTROKE DEPRESSION

Mr. C, a 69-year-old attorney, suffered a brief spell of weakness and facial asymmetry, recovering after a few minutes without sequelae. A CAT scan revealed a small basal ganglia infarct that rapidly resolved over the next two months. Mr. C, however, became distressingly preoccupied with death; he began to lose interest in his work and reported difficulties eating and sleeping. His family noted that he was more quiet than usual, socially withdrawn, and intermittently irritable. At the suggestion of his wife, he sought psychiatric treatment.

During the initial interview, Mr. C's depression was quite apparent. He looked dejected, spoke slowly and quietly, and sighed frequently. There were no tears and he was not suicidal, but he admitted to feeling hopeless and extremely pessimistic. Although the infarct had resolved without apparent consequences, he remained apprehensive and continued to watch anxiously for signs of a recurrence. As the evaluation progressed, it became apparent that Mr. C had been suffering from a milder form of depression for nearly 10 years. He movingly described long-standing feelings of professional inadequacy and how he had failed to live up to his own expectations of himself as a lawyer. He had never mentioned these feelings to anyone, not even his wife. Rather, over the years, he had tried to combat his depression by undertaking a vigorous exercise regimen and by taking a variety of over-the-counter medications such as aspirin and nonsteroidal antiinflammatory drugs. With the onset of the stroke, he became unable to exercise, and this contributed to his burgeoning obsession with physical debilitation and death. In older people, it is not unusual to observe symptoms and sequelae of a medical illness blending into preexisting negative personality characteristics or reactivating prior depression, so that a simple cause for the current depression cannot be easily uncovered. Because of these complicated and intermingling factors leading to the depression, it is also more difficult to prescribe a therapeutic approach than in the case of an uncomplicated depression.

Mr. C was treated with psychotherapy, along with an antidepressant. Over the ensuing weeks of psychotherapy, he began to explore long-standing feelings of conflict and competition with his wife, as well as buried rage at various colleagues and legal organizations that had never acknowledged his achievements. With effective medication and discussion of these long-standing conflicts, Mr. C's depression began to lift, and he has remained depression-free on maintenance medication up to the time of writing this account.

In addition to neurological disorders, other medical conditions associated with depression in late life include cardiovascular illness, endocrine disorders, and cancer. Major depression occurs in nearly one-fourth of post-myocardial infarction (MI) patients, and the mortality rate is increased in post-MI patients who are depressed. As many as half of all patients undergoing coronary artery bypass surgery will suffer from depressive disorders.

Depression is a common component of adrenal dysfunction, both hyperadrenalism (Cushing's syndrome) and hypoadrenalism (Addison's disease). Both hyper- and hypothyroidism are associated with depression. Hyperthyroid states in the elderly can produce a condition known as "apathetic thyrotoxicosis," in which the thyroid function is elevated but the behavioral manifestations are characterized by reduced energy, apathy, and indifference. Depression may develop as part of hypoparathyroidism as well.

Depressive disorders commonly occur in association with cancer and other chronic severe disorders, although the association is not higher in older people. The prevalence of depression ranges from 50% (cancer of the pancreas) to 25% (colon) to 11% (gastric). Depression is common with chronic pain syndromes, chronic arthritis, chronic fatigue syndrome, and vitamin deficiencies, especially vitamin B_{12} and folic acid.

Since depression and physical illness so often coexist, a physical examination is an essential early part of any psychiatric diagnostic evaluation. Laboratory tests should also be performed, since there may be hidden metabolic or endocrine disorders that can be treated to relieve the depression. These are discussed on page 33.

MASKED DEPRESSION

Some older people suffering from physical symptoms may be unaware of being depressed or are unable to express feelings of despondency. Suppressed emotions are sometimes more acceptably experienced as physical symptoms, a condition termed **masked depression**. Clinicians, especially family practitioners, gastroenterologists, rheumatologists, and pain specialists, commonly encounter depressed older people who claim to suffer solely from a physical disorder, as in the following case.

THE CASE OF MR. D: MASKED DEPRESSION

Mr. D had just retired at age 65 with no plans for how he would spend his time. Now, sitting in his physician's office, his eyes were moist, his facial expression sad, and his movements slow. He denied all feelings of depression but reported a constant burning sensation in his stomach. Mr. D underwent extensive physical examination and a number of diagnostic tests. Even after all of his tests proved negative and he was pronounced to be in good physical health, he could not believe that there was no underlying serious illness causing the distressing burning sensation in his stomach, sour taste in his mouth, flatulence, and fluctuating appetite.

Mr. D was referred to a psychiatrist who, through careful questioning about his childhood, learned of the many deaths that had occurred in his family when Mr. D was a young boy. It further emerged that the onset of his stomach symptoms coincided with several recent, unexpected deaths of close friends. He was started on antidepressant medication. In psychotherapy sessions, he began to discuss his long-suppressed feelings of grief about these many losses. As the therapy progressed, the burning stomach sensation and other symptoms gradually disappeared.

DELUSIONAL DEPRESSION

A particularly severe form of late-life depression includes delusional thinking. The diagnosis of delusional depression, also known as psychotic depression, is usually readily apparent, since virtually all patients have clear-cut signs of a major depressive disorder in addition to delusions. Typical delusions associated with late-life depression are shown in Table 2.4.

Delusional depression is usually not difficult to diagnose, but it may be particularly difficult to treat. Since delusionally depressed older patients deny the illness, having attributed all symptoms to a delusional belief, it is not unusual for them to refuse treatment or comply poorly

TABLE 2.4. Delusions Associated with Late-Life Depressions

Type of delusion	Example
Nihilistic	1. "I'm hopeless."
	2. "Don't treat me, Doctor. Spend your time with someone more deserving or who can benefit."
	3. "I'm broke; all my money is gone."
Somatic	1. "My stomach/brain/heart/bladder is sick/diseased/missing."
	2. "I have cancer that nobody is telling me about."
	3. "I have butterflies in my skin" (café au lait spots of aging).
Paranoid	1. "I'm being punished because I have lived a bad life."
	2. "My children hate me" (not always a delusion).
	3. "I'm being controlled/watched/manipulated."
	4. "He/she/they want sex with me."

with treatment that has been started. Hospitalization becomes necessary when the severe sleep and appetite disturbances lead to life-threatening states of exhaustion, weight loss, electrolyte imbalance, pneumonia, and cardiac arrhythmias.

DEPRESSION AND DEMENTIA

Depression exacerbates the normal decline in concentration and memory that accompanies aging, and it is not unusual for patients and family members to mistake the cognitive impairment of a depressive disorder for developing Alzheimer's disease. On the other hand, depression is a common feature of true dementia (see Chapter 6). Depressive symptoms may be present in as many as 8 out of 10 patients with Alzheimer's disease (Lararus et al., 1987), although the degree of symptomatology may vary from mild depression to the severe emotional lability that typically accompanies the late stages of Alzheimer's disease.

Guidelines for distinguishing between the cognitive impairment of depression versus Alzheimer's disease are summarized in Table 2.5.

TABLE 2.5. Cognitive Impairment Associated with Depression versus Dementia

Cognitive functioning	Depression	Dementia
1. Memory complaint (subjective)	Patient complains constantly about memory impairment	Patient tries to cover up the memory impairment
2. Memory function (objective)	Mild, and rarely as severe as the patient's complaints would suggest	Very severe, but either dismissed by the patient or excused (confabulation)
3. Orientation	Good	Impaired
4. Reasoning	Preserved	Obviously impaired

Questioning loved ones and caregivers about the duration and severity of the cognitive decline is also helpful in discriminating between the two disorders.

The following case illustrates the beneficial effect of antidepressants on late-life depression, anxiety, and the loss of memory.

THE CASE OF DR. E: DEPRESSION MASQUERADING AS DEMENTIA

A 78-year-old physician had struggled with depression throughout her life. During medical school, internship, and residency, Dr. E recalled feeling constantly anxious about her inadequate performance compared with other students. In conjunction with psychotherapy, a variety of antidepressants was tried over the years. Each treatment produced a reaction of depressive symptoms, and each was then discontinued because of side effects.

The pattern of frequent, brief treatment-responsive depressions continued into old age, when Dr. E began to notice memory lapses. Now semiretired, she could not recall her patients' histories with her former ease. Worrying that her memory impairment would interfere with her functions as a physician, she sometimes became so distressed that she experienced periods of crying, irritability, and poor sleep. Finally, her colleagues suggested that she should discontinue practicing medicine and seek consultation.

During the consultation, Dr. E was clearly despondent, distracted, highly anxious, and fidgety. She reported very poor sleep, erratic appetite, and a sense of hopelessness. But most of her complaints centered around her memory loss. Like many others her age, she had terrible difficulties remembering names and finding words when she was speaking. She misplaced common household objects and garments, could not recall what she had read in the newspaper, and was unable to balance her checkbook. She was diagnosed as having a depression; an antidepressant medication and psychotherapy were begun.

Two months later, Dr. E was remarkably well groomed, articulate, and alert. She actively engaged in the psychotherapy and appeared neither depressed nor anxious. Most notably, there was no apparent evidence of memory loss. She was well oriented, able to draw a picture of a clock face (a common, simple office test for dementia), and to repeat a series of numbers forward and backward.

This patient, who had suffered from lifelong bouts of depression, did not have a dementing illness. Rather, her memory loss was caused by a late-life depression. When her depression lifted following treatment with effective medication, her cognitive functioning was commensurate with that of her age group.

MEDICATIONS THAT CAUSE OR WORSEN DEPRESSION

Many medications taken by older people for common late-life illnesses may initiate or worsen a preexisting depression. For example, some antihypertensives cause low energy, listlessness, lack of initiative, and excessive fatigue. Medications that can induce or worsen depression are listed in Table 2.6.

TABLE 2.6. Medications That Cause or Worsen Depression

*Alpha-methyldopa	Guanethidine
Anabolic steroids	HMGCoA inhibitors
Baclofen	L-Dopa
*Barbiturates	Metoclopramide
Benzodiazepines	Neuroleptics
Calcium channel blockers	Nonsteroidal antiinflammatory
Cimetidine, ranitidine,	agents
and other H2 blockers	Opiate analgesics
*Clonidine	*Progesterone
Cycloserine	Propranolol and other beta
Cyclosporine	blockers
Digitalis	*Reserpine
Disulfiram	Sulfonamides
Ethambutol	Thiazide diuretics
*Glucocorticoids	

Note. Drugs most likely to induce or worsen are indicated by an asterisk (*). Data from Salzman (1998).

ANTIDEPRESSANT MEDICATIONS

Since antidepressants were first discovered in the late 1950s and early 1960s, approximately two dozen different medications have become available for treatment of depressive symptoms. Because only a few of these drugs have been specifically tested in elderly people, most of the information about their effectiveness is based on research in young and middle-aged adults. Despite this lack of research, clinical experience with elderly patients indicates the following:

- Antidepressants are as effective for elderly people who are depressed as they are for young and middle-aged adults.
- As a group, older people are more sensitive to the pharmacological properties of antidepressant drugs and are more likely to develop side effects.
- For these reasons, physicians usually start older patients at doses lower than those commonly used for young and middle-aged adults, and then increase doses more slowly. The prescribing maxim that physicians should follow when prescribing for this age group is "Start low, and go slow."
- Although older people usually respond to lower antidepressant doses, some need the same doses as young and middle-aged adults.
- Since effective doses vary from person to person, prescribers, elderly patients, and their families need to work together to find the most effective dose with the fewest side effects. This may take time.
- Many older patients take longer than younger and middle-aged adults to achieve the full therapeutic benefit of antidepressants. Experienced clinicians know it can take 8 to 12 weeks for an older patient to feel significantly less depressed. Physicians should resist discontinuing or changing a medication prematurely in the mistaken belief that it is not effective.

Prescribers also need to ascertain if the patient is using substances such as tobacco or alcohol. Cigarette smoking decreases therapeutic effects by inducing the metabolism of antidepressants. Alcohol makes depressed patients feel worse over time because of its depressant effects on the central nervous system. However, since the short-term effect of alcohol relieves depressive symptoms for a few hours, depressed elders may increase their alcohol consumption, thereby significantly worsening preexisting depressive symptoms. Older patients may not realize that they have increased their alcohol intake to dangerous levels, or may attempt to cover up their drinking by denial. Information from family and caregivers is sometimes very useful in evaluating recent changes in alcohol intake.

INDICATIONS AND CONTRAINDICATIONS FOR ANTIDEPRESSANT MEDICATION

Although some older patients become depressed for the first time after age 65 (known as **late-onset depression**), many have had prior depressions. It appears that older patients who have had prior depressions (called **early-onset depression** to distinguish it from depressions after age 65) do not respond to antidepressant medications quite as well as those older patients whose depression appears for the first time in late life (Alexopoulos et al., 1996). Older people with early-onset depressions often need specialized treatment by a geriatric psychiatrist or psychopharmacologist.

It is also important to know whether the depressed older person has had any previous manic symptoms or a diagnosis of bipolar disorder. The diagnosis and treatment of depression in older people with bipolar disorder is discussed on page 58.

It is very helpful to have an accurate picture of any family history of depressions before initiating treatment. Such information is not always readily available, however, since depression was not always recognized by previous generations. Family tales of relatives who spent prolonged periods in bed, often went to physicians or hospitals, were unable to work, or drank excessive alcohol may be indicative of a family history of depression. It is also helpful to determine whether the patient's children or grandchildren have experienced depression. A positive response by family members to a particular antidepressant may suggest its use in the patient, since family members sometimes respond similarly to a particular medication.

An antidepressant should not be prescribed without a physical examination or approval from the patient's physician. Essential pretreatment laboratory tests (Table 2.7) should also be conducted. If tricyclic antidepressants are being considered, an electrocardiogram is also necessary, since these drugs alter cardiac conduction (see section on tricyclics).

RECOVERY FROM DEPRESSION

Some depressed older patients imagine that they will never feel any less depressed, fatigued, apathetic, hopeless, and worthless. Some may not even remember that there was a time in their lives when they did not feel depressed. It is not uncommon to hear an elder comment about having been born depressed and having stayed that way throughout life.

Older depressed individuals are understandably impatient, hoping that an antidepressant medication will work like an aspirin for headaches: one or two pills and they will feel better. In general, however, antidepressants take several weeks or even 1 to 3 months before improvement occurs. The earliest sign of response is usually improved sleep, followed by increased attention to clothes and grooming (which may have been neglected during the depressive period). Women begin to brush their hair; men start to shave again. Even in these early stages of improvement, however, the older person's mood may still be depressed, and a question such as "How are you feeling?" can elicit sighs,

TABLE 2.7. Medical Tests for Antidepressant Treatment

- Tests of thyroid function (T_3, T_4, TSH)
- Electrocardiogram (EKG)
- Folic acid and vitamin B_{12} levels
- CBC, liver function tests

shrugs, and negative responses of hopelessness, pointlessness, and use-lessness. Some people feel better for a short period of time and then seem to slip back, before feeling better again. The slow and irregular response of older people to the therapeutic benefits of antidepressants is illustrated in the following case.

THE CASE OF MRS. F: "IF AT FIRST YOU DON'T SUCCEED . . . "

Mrs. F, 77 years old, was referred for treatment of a depression that had not responded to antidepressant medication. She was a charming and quite talkative woman who moved slowly, using a walker, but was otherwise not physically compromised. She would chat amiably in the office, with no hint of depression, until she was specifically asked about her mood and whether she felt sad. Inevitably, her eyes filling with tears, her voice would drop to an inaudible level and her entire demeanor would convey severe depression. Mrs. F admitted that she was worried about having Alzheimer's disease, although there was no evidence of dementia. She was, however, quite anxious and would fidget in her chair, sigh frequently, and play with her hair or the hem of her dress. She described being apprehensive, frightened at night, and "wor-ried all the time." Elderly people with depression are often also very anxious; in many cases, the combination of anxiety and de-pression makes it difficult to determine whether the patient is suf-fering from an anxiety disorder with added depression, or a de-pressive disorder with added anxiety.

The ineffective antidepressant prescribed for Mrs. F by an-other physician was gradually tapered over a 2-week period and then discontinued. An antidepressant from a different class was in-troduced over the following 3 weeks, but Mrs. F seemed consid-erably more depressed. Her physician, concerned for her well-being, began to consider hospitalization. Although by the fourth week she seemed brighter and less anxious, her feeling of depres-sion did not diminish, and she even commented that the preced-ing week had been the worst of all. Two factors are worth noting here: First, antidepressants often reduce anxiety as well as depres-sion; and second, depressed people can show early signs of im-provement in energy, appetite, sleep, and grooming without actu-ally feeling any less depressed.

In subsequent weeks, Mrs. F's improvement continued and

by week 6, she thought she was feeling a little better; by week 8, she was certain that she was feeling better, an assessment with which the clinician concurred.

TREATMENT DURATION

How long should an older person stay on antidepressant medication once the depression has disappeared? This commonly asked question does not have a simple answer. Many research studies indicate that depression is an illness that recurs when patients are not maintained on antidepressant medication after the depression has lifted (Reynolds, Perel, Frank, et al., 1999). Elders who have had previous depressions may need to take medications indefinitely in order to prevent relapse or the development of another depression. As many as 90% of patients will relapse if they discontinue antidepressant treatment too soon.

The decision to maintain antidepressant medication is based on a number of factors, including the severity of the depression, the number of prior depressions, as well as side effects caused by the treatment. If medication has been helpful and has not produced any significant side effects, then it is obviously easier to recommend that it be continued even when depressed symptoms are no longer present. Some elders, however, do not wish to continue to take medication, especially when they are feeling better. Nevertheless, physicians should encourage these patients to continue antidepressant medication for 6 to 12 months *after the depression has resolved*. For those older individuals who have had a severe depression or prior depressions, it may be necessary to continue taking antidepressants more or less indefinitely, reducing the dose if side effects develop. Maintenance doses of antidepressant medication may also have to be reduced as the older person continues to age.

OVERVIEW OF ANTIDEPRESSANT MEDICATIONS

There are four classes of antidepressant medications, based on their effects in the brain:

- Tricyclic antidepressants (TCAs; sometimes called heterocyclic antidepressants).
- Selective serotonin reuptake inhibitors (SSRIs; sometimes called serotonin reuptake inhibitors, SRIs).
- Monoamine oxidase inhibitors (MAOIs).
- Atypical antidepressants, which comprise a growing miscellaneous group of new antidepressants that do not easily fit into one of the other three pharmacological categories.

Antidepressants work by enhancing the function of neurotransmitters. It is likely that depression is caused by a highly complex and intricate change in sensitivity of receptors for these neurotransmitters rather than quantity of neurotransmitter present in the brain. Two neurotransmitters, norepinephrine and serotonin, are particularly associated with depression, and one or both are affected by virtually all antidepressant drugs. But other neurotransmitters, peptides, and hormones may also play a role in depression and be affected by these antidepressants. The classes of drugs and their effects on brain neurochemistry are shown in Table 2.8 on pages 38–39.

TRICYCLIC ANTIDEPRESSANTS (TCAs)

TCAs (sometimes called **heterocyclic antidepressants**) were first introduced into clinical medicine in the late 1950s. Essential information regarding their effects can be summarized from a large body of research and clinical experience:

- TCAs are very efficacious for depression in elderly people.
- They are also effective in preventing relapse and recurrence.
- Blood levels of some TCAs can be measured and used as guidelines to adjust daily dosages (see page 37).
- TCAs are no longer used as frequently to treat depression because of their side effects. Although mitigated by low doses, side effects still commonly occur and often cause considerable discomfort for older patients.
- These drugs may take as long as 12 weeks to produce a full

therapeutic effect, although most older patients begin to experience some benefit within 1 month.

Initiating Treatment with TCAs

It is especially important to obtain an EKG prior to administration of TCAs because high blood levels of this class of antidepressants sometimes cause arrhythmias or heart block. During treatment, the development of these cardiac conduction irregularities can be detected by repeat EKGs (see section on cardiac effects).

Using Blood Levels of TCAs to Guide Dosing

Blood levels correlate with clinical response for three of the most commonly prescribed TCAs—imipramine, desipramine, and nortriptyline—and can help clinicians determine whether to alter the dose (see Table 2.9 on page 40).

TCAs are metabolized by cytochrome P450 enzymes in the liver, producing **hydroxymetabolites**. High blood levels of hydroxymetabolites may cause serious cardiac side effects, including potentially lethal cardiac arrhythmias. Since blood levels of hydroxymetabolites are not measured by routine laboratory tests, it is necessary to monitor their levels indirectly using the EKG (see section on cardiac side effects).

Blood levels of TCAs may be elevated by concomitant administration of medications that inhibit cytochrome P450 enzymatic metabolism (see page 50). Repeat blood levels, as well as EKGs, may be necessary to ensure that levels do not alter cardiac conduction when these drug interactions are anticipated.

Side Effects of TCAs

Like many useful medications, the therapeutic benefits of TCAs are sometimes accompanied by unwanted side effects, especially in very old people. In many cases, the appearance as well as the severity of TCA side effects correlate very closely with the dosage and blood levels of tricyclics. Simply lowering the dose may reduce the side effects, making it possible for the older patient to continue taking these useful

TABLE 2.8. Drug Classes and Their Effects on Brain Neurochemistry

Class of drug	Generic name	Trade name	Effect on brain neurochemistry
1. Tricyclic or heterocyclic antidepressants	Amitriptyline Amoxapine Clomipramine Desipramine Doxepin Imipramine Nortriptyline Protriptyline Trimipramine	Elavil Asendin Anafranil Norpramin Sinequan Tofranil Pamelor Vivactil Surmontil	Increase both norepinephrine and serotonin by blocking presynaptic reuptake.
2. SSRIs	Citalopram Fluoxetine Fluvoxamine Paroxetine Sertraline	Celexa Prozac Luvox Paxil Zoloft	Exclusively increase serotonin function by blocking presynaptic reuptake.
3. MAOIs	Phenelzine Tranylcypromine	Nardil Parnate	Increase both norepinephrine and serotonin by blocking their metabolism.

4. Miscellaneous			
a. Serotonin and norepinephrine uptake blocker	Venlafaxine	Effexor	Primarily acts as an SSRI. At doses greater than 100 mg/day, norepinephrine reuptake is also inhibited.
b. Postsynaptic serotonin activity	Nefazodone	Serzone	Weak serotonin reuptake inhibitor but strongly blocks postsynaptic serotonin receptor.
c. Postsynaptic serotonin activity	Mirtazapine	Remeron	Blocks postsynaptic receptor—stimulated by both presynaptic norepinephrine and serotonin.
d. Dopamine and norepinephrine	Bupropion	Wellbutrin	Actual antidepressant mechanism not well understood; blocks presynaptic norepinephrine and dopamine reuptake.

**TABLE 2.9. Correlation between Blood Levels
and Therapeutic Response**

Drug	Therapeutic blood range	Type of correlation
Imipramine	75–150 ng/ml	"Sigmoidal": Blood levels above therapeutic range do not further increase response.
Desipramine	75–150 ng/ml	"Sigmoidal": Blood levels above therapeutic range do not further increase response.
Nortriptyline	25–150 ng/ml	"Therapeutic window": Response decreases beyond maximum therapeutic range.

medications. The most common side effects are sedation, orthostatic hypotension, and anticholinergic side effects.

Sedation most often develops at the beginning of treatment, when it may actually be welcomed by patients, since sleep becomes longer and more restful. However, after several days or weeks, the older person may start to feel sleepy in the morning hours and even into the afternoon. In order to avoid daytime sedation (caused by the antihistamine properties of these drugs), clinicians often instruct patients to take the daily dose at bedtime. Since concurrent use of other antihistamine and sedating medications will increase daytime drowsiness, they should be avoided.

Orthostatic hypotension (a sudden decrease in blood pressure causing lightheadedness or dizziness when getting out of bed or standing up) is not unusual in older patients who take TCAs. Although usually transient, this can cause an older person to fall, thereby heightening the risk of fractures due to increased bone fragility in old age. Caregivers should constantly remind the older patient to rise slowly from a seated position, and when getting out of bed, to first sit on the edge of the bed for a few seconds before standing up, especially when going to the bathroom in the middle of the night. Orthostatic hypotension may also occur when climbing stairs or exercising. Slower, deliberate movements can help avoid this side effect.

Anticholinergic side effects (the decrease or blocking of the mucosal moisturizing effect of acetylcholine) result in dry mouth, constipation, difficulty urinating, and blurred vision, all of which seriously impair the older person's quality of life. With dry mouth, dentures fit less well and porcelain fillings loosen, making it difficult to eat and enjoy food. Constipation may lead to impaction serious enough to require medical intervention; blurred vision can interfere with the ability to read or watch television. Anticholinergic side effects also aggravate symptoms of an enlarged prostate gland in men. It is important, therefore, that these side effects be reported to the prescribing clinicians as soon as they begin to develop. In many cases, simply lowering the dose will be helpful. The following case illustrates the development of a serious anticholinergic side effect of antidepressant medication in an older individual.

THE CASE OF MRS. G: ANTICHOLINERGIC OVERLOAD

Mrs. G, a 76-year-old woman in good physical health, who was successfully taking maintenance doses of a tricyclic, developed a bad case of the flu one February. Her doctor prescribed a cough medicine that contained codeine, a cough suppressant with anticholinergic properties, to treat her constant coughing and lack of sleep. The cough rapidly subsided and Mrs. G was able to sleep. Because it was so helpful, she decided to take an extra teaspoon or two to speed her recovery, and, without her doctor's permission or knowledge, she increased her dose. Two days later, Mrs. G developed a high fever, appearing ashen to her friends. They rushed her to a hospital emergency room where an X ray of her abdomen indicated that she had cancer blocking her intestines. Mrs. G's son received a midnight call informing him that emergency surgery to remove a portion of his mother's small intestine was about to be performed. The son, a physician, told the surgeon of Mrs. G's treatment with the tricyclic and her recent need for codeine cough medicine. He suggested that the medication be stopped and the surgery withheld pending further observation. Later that evening, a nurse gave Mrs. G a mild laxative. Shortly following a bowel movement, her fever subsided, and she no longer looked faint. In the morning a repeat X ray showed no further bowel obstruction and no evidence of cancer, and Mrs. G was discharged, her healthy small intestine still intact.

Mrs. G had not only failed to take her cough medication exactly as prescribed, but she also had not told her doctor that she was taking a TCA. Since both medications had strong anticholinergic properties, Mrs. G experienced severe gastrointestinal anticholinergic side effects that transiently paralyzed her bowel, caused a high fever, and left her weak. Had not a vigilant nurse attempted to relieve Mrs. G's constipation, she might have undergone major surgery that was totally unnecessary. This case illustrates how important it is for a physician to have a complete list of a patient's medications, even of something as seemingly inconsequential as cough medicine, before making a diagnosis or recommending a medical or surgical procedure. Physicians should also be aware that some elders do not consider over-the-counter remedies to be medications. It is therefore necessary to specifically inquire about all medicines, herbs, vitamins, and other health preparations that are purchased without a prescription.

Acetylcholine also plays an important role in memory, attention, and concentration. Beginning at about age 50, acetylcholine in the central nervous system begins to gradually decline, causing increased forgetfulness. Beyond age 50, the normal aging process progressively decreases acetylcholine production, which results in increasingly impaired memory functioning. In dementia, acetylcholine is virtually absent from some parts of the brain.

TCAs further impair memory by compounding the age-related decline in acetylcholine. For this reason, therapeutic doses are usually low enough to cause only a slight worsening of memory. While high doses of TCAs are almost always deleterious to the memory, its therapeutic antidepressant properties will sometimes improve memory function as the depression begins to resolve, since depression itself may interfere with memory.

Anticholinergic toxicity may develop when an older patient who is taking a TCA also takes several other medications that have anticholinergic properties. Polypharmacy, as described in Chapter 1, typically occurs during treatment for a medical disorder, or during recovery from a surgical procedure. For example, the popular pain medication, Demerol, has strong anticholinergic effects, and Lomotil, commonly used for gastrointestinal disorders, also has marked anticholinergic properties. When these medications are given in conjunction with a TCA to a depressed older person recovering from gastrointestinal surgery, serious acetylcholine diminution can develop, culminating in anticholinergic toxicity. This very serious condition includes the following symptoms:

- Confusion
- Disorientation
- Agitation
- Seriously impaired recent memory
- Markedly impaired concentration
- Paranoid thinking
- Visual hallucinations

Any of these symptoms in an older person taking a TCA may be indicative of anticholinergic toxicity. The following case illustrates central nervous system anticholinergic toxicity that resulted in an erroneous diagnosis.

THE CASE OF MR. H: ANTICHOLINERGIC DELIRIUM

Mr. H, a 78-year-old retired schoolteacher, was recovering in an intensive care unit following major surgery for stomach cancer. Because he had been depressed and sleeping poorly before the surgery, a TCA with sedating and strong anticholinergic properties was prescribed. Following the surgery, he was given Demerol for pain and Lomotil to quiet his intestinal tract. Two days after surgery, Mr. H wryly commented to his visiting daughter, "There should not be bugs crawling on the wall in a hospital as good as this one." His daughter gently reassured him that there were no bugs crawling on the wall, kissed him goodnight, and went home for the evening. Later that night, convinced that all the hospital personnel were trying to harm him, Mr. H began screaming, threatened the nurses and, pulling the tubes out of his arms, tried to climb out of bed. He had to be restrained.

Having learned of this behavior the following morning, the surgeon informed the family that Mr. H's psychotic behavior was a sign that the cancer had metastasized to his brain, and that he would die within a short period of time. Mr. H's physician daughter, aware of the anticholinergic effects of the various medications that were being prescribed, suggested that they be discontinued. Two days later, Mr. H no longer saw bugs on the wall and was no longer confused, agitated, fearful, or paranoid. There were no brain metastases, and he lived for another 2 years, never experiencing a recurrence of these symptoms.

Mr. H's episode was an acute anticholingeric delirium brought about by a combination of anticholinergic medications, and, like Mrs. G's case, illustrates the importance of withholding a diagnosis until drug side effects have been ruled out as a possible cause of an older patient's symptoms.

Serious anticholinergic toxicity rarely arises when a TCA is taken alone at therapeutic doses. Medications with the potential of producing this side effect when prescribed at the same time as tricyclics are shown in Table 2.10.

TCAs have quinidine-like properties that affect cardiac rate and rhythm depending on the dose and amount of drug that reaches the heart tissue. Therapeutic doses stabilize heart conduction, but higher doses, like quinidine, can cause a disruption of regular heartbeat, leading to tachycardia, block, atrial arrhythmias, and even potentially lethal ventricular arrhythmias. Older patients, especially those with heart disease, are likely to be more susceptible to these cardiac side effects. As discussed earlier in this chapter, a baseline EKG should always be taken before TCA treatment is started and repeated as the dose is increased, especially above 150 mg/day. Palpitations, skipped beats, heart flutter, and tachycardia indicate a repeat electrocardiogram. Widening of the QRS or QT_c interval compared with baseline is an early warning sign that the TCA or the hydroxymetabolite is adversely affecting the heart. At this point, the dose should be decreased until the EKG returns to its baseline measurement. It is advisable to consult a cardiologist for further dosing guidelines should this effect develop.

TABLE 2.10. Medications with Strong Anticholinergic Side Effects

Medication	Primary indication

Anticholinergic drugs
    Artane (trihexyphenidyl)
    Cogentin (benztropine)
    Kemadrin (procyclidine)
	Antiparkinsonian antiviral; treat neuroleptic side effects

Codeine	Pain, cough
Cystospaz (hyoscyamine)	Urinary smooth muscle spasm
Demerol (meperidine)	Pain
Donnatal (hyoscyamine + atropine + scopolamine)	Gastrointestinal spasm + motility
Flexeril (cyclobenzaprine)	Muscle spasm
Levsin, Levsinex (hyoscyamine sulfate)	Peptic ulcer, gastrointestinal spasm
Lomotil (atropine sulfate)	Diarrhea
Neuroleptics	Psychosis, agitation
Symmetrel (amantadine)	Parkinson's disease
Tricyclic antidepressants	Depression, panic, phobias
Urised (methenamine)	Urinary smooth muscle spasm

Recommended TCAs for Older Patients

All TCAs, divided into two broad categories based on their tertiary amine tricylics or secondary amine chemical structure, are effective medications. As a general rule, tertiary amines have more serious (especially anticholinergic) side effects and are not recommended for older patients. Examples of tertiary amine tricyclic antidepressants are the following:

- Elavil (amitriptyline)
- Tofranil (imipramine)

- Sinequan (doxepin)
- Anafranil (clomipramine)
- Surmontil (trimipramine)

Two secondary amine tricyclics also possess anticholinergic properties that limit their usefulness: Vivactil (protriptyline) and Asendin (amoxapine).

Norpramin (desipramine), and Pamelor (nortriptyline), prescribed almost exclusively for older patients, are safe and effective secondary amines. Both drugs have the advantage of producing relatively modest side effects compared with tertiary amines and are also useful because their blood levels can be accurately measured and utilized in making dose adjustments (see Table 2.9).

Although blood tests may be useful in monitoring tricyclic blood levels, no specific doses or blood levels are consistently therapeutic. Research has shown that the therapeutic range of plasma levels in older individuals does not differ from that necessary for clinical improvement in younger adults (Nelson, Mazure, & Jatlow, 1995). However, because the aging process slows the metabolism of drugs, older patients often reach therapeutic plasma levels at lower doses than younger patients. For this reason, it is important for the physician to maintain frequent communication with the patient, family, or caregiver during the first few weeks of treatment so that doses can be kept as low as possible and adjusted if side effects appear. Doses of Norpramin and Pamelor for the older patient are shown in Table 2.11.

TABLE 2.11. Geriatric Dosages for TCAs

Name of drug	Starting dose	Therapeutic dose range
Norpramin (desipramine)	10–25 mg/day	25–150 mg/day
Pamelor (nortriptyline)	10–25 mg/day	25–100 mg/day

SELECTIVE SEROTONIN
REUPTAKE INHIBITORS (SSRIs)

The SSRI antidepressants—Prozac (fluoxetine), Zoloft (sertraline), Paxil (paroxetine), Luvox (fluvoxamine), and Celexa (citalopram)—have become the most widely used antidepressants in the United States as well as other parts of the world. Since they do not cause orthostatic hypotension or anticholinergic side effects, they are particularly well suited for elderly depressed individuals. Evidence suggests that SSRI antidepressants are as efficacious as TCAs for depressed older patients regardless of the degree of depression. Some physicians, however, still prefer to prescribe tricyclics for severe depressions and SSRIs for depressions that are mild or moderately severe.

While doses of SSRIs used to treat elderly patients are usually lower than those used to treat younger adults, there is no evidence to suggest that one SSRI is more or less effective than any other. As a class, they share similar side effects, although there are minor differences among the drugs. Common SSRI side effects include agitation or drowsiness, weight gain or loss, and bruising easily. In general, these are mild, related to dosage levels, and usually do not interfere with the older individual's daily life or health.

As with the TCAs, the older patient must continue to take the SSRI as prescribed once the therapeutic dosage is reached, continuing even after the depression lifts in order to prevent relapse.

Noncompliance is less likely with SSRIs than tricyclics, because SSRI side effects are not as frequent, as annoying, or as serious. However, SSRIs are typically more expensive, and older patients with fixed, limited financial resources may not be able to purchase the medication on a long-term basis. Family members and doctors need to be aware of this possibility in order to avoid relapse or recurrence of the depression.

Prozac (fluoxetine)

Prozac was the first SSRI antidepressant to become available in the United States, and it has become one of the most widely prescribed antidepressants in the world. Prozac has a longer elimination half-life than other SSRIs, which is both an advantage and a disadvantage for the elderly person. Because of its long duration of action, an occasional missed dose is not likely to produce a significant worsening or relapse. However, if side effects develop and Prozac is discontinued, it takes a longer time for its effects to disappear.

The starting dose for Prozac is 10 mg/day, and the usual therapeutic dose is 10 or 20 mg/day, the pill being taken just once a day. However, some very elderly or extremely frail depressed older people become agitated on only 10 mg/day. For these individuals, even lower starting doses may be obtained by using a liquid form of the drug (unfortunately, not very pleasant to the taste). This can be poured into a measuring cup to provide starting doses of 2–5 mg/day that can be gradually increased to 10 mg, after which the medication may be taken in pill form.

Recent experience has suggested that estrogen replacement therapy for postmenopausal women may enhance the response of some elderly depressed women to Prozac (Schneider et al., 1997).

Zoloft (sertraline)

Zoloft is an effective antidepressant with modest and relatively infrequent side effects. An advantage of this SSRI is its broad therapeutic dose range, from 25–150 mg/day. For the frail and very elderly depressed person, starting doses are as low as 12.5 mg but more typically are 25 mg. Most older patients begin to feel less depressed when daily doses reach 100–150 mg/day. Neither agitation nor sedation are frequent side effects of Zoloft, but upset stomach, bloating, and diarrhea are common early in treatment.

Paxil (paroxetine)

Paxil is the only drug in this class that has been studied in individuals 75 years or older (Mulsant et al., 1999). Its effects are not significantly different from other SSRIs, although it is unique in having very mild anticholinergic properties. Some older patients who take Paxil develop mild constipation, dry mouth, blurred vision, or trouble starting urination. In most instances, these symptoms are transient. Paxil tends to be sedating and, for some individuals, is best taken at bedtime. In patients 75 years and older, there is no observable increase in memory loss.

Luvox (fluvoxamine)

Luvox, like Zoloft, has the advantage of a broad therapeutic dosage range (25–100 mg/day), and the two share similar side effects. Compared with other SSRI antidepressants, however, there is relatively little research experience in treating elderly patients.

Celexa (citalopram)

This newest SSRI antidepressant has frequently been given to depressed older patients with significant success. Like Prozac, Celexa has a longer half-life than Zoloft, Paxil, or Luvox. While its side-effect profile has not been shown to differ from that of the other SSRIs, Celexa is unique in not having clinically significant interactions with other medications (see next section).

Starting doses and dosage ranges of SSRIs are summarized in Table 2.12.

Drug Interactions with SSRI Antidepressants

SSRIs, unlike the TCAs, may interfere with the cytochrome P450 hepatic metabolism of other medications. Although the cytochrome

TABLE 2.12. SSRI Starting Doses and Dosage Ranges

Drug	Starting dose	Recommended daily dose
Prozac (fluoxetine)	5–10 mg/day	10–20 mg/day
Zoloft (sertraline)	12.5–25 mg/day	25–100 mg/day
Paxil (paroxetine)	5–10 mg/day	10–20 mg/day
Luvox (fluvoxamine)	25–50 mg/day	50–100 mg/day
Celexa (citalopram)	10–20 mg/day	20–40 mg/day

enzymes are only slightly affected by the normal aging process, their activity may be substantially decreased by illnesses such as hepatitis, cancer, AIDS, and cirrhosis. Some medications also alter the function of these enzymes, either inhibiting or increasing their ability to metabolize (see Appendix).

Modern psychiatry is now very knowledgeable about the effects of particular medications on cytochrome enzyme metabolism. Most drugs are metabolized by members of the cytochrome P450 (CP-450) class of enzymes. Within this class are many distinct subfamilies of isoenzymes, each (alone or in combination with others) responsible for metabolizing certain drugs. The isoenzymes that are especially important in metabolizing antidepressants and other psychotropic medications are 2D6, 1A2, 3A4, and, to a lesser extent, 2C19. For example, Prozac and Paxil are predominantly metabolized by the CP450 isoenzyme 2D6, whereas Zoloft is metabolized primarily by 3A4. When a cytochrome enzyme is decreased by illness or by a medication, other medications that are usually metabolized by this enzyme begin to accumulate and cause side effects. For example, Prozac (fluoxetine) and Paxil (paroxetine) inhibit the CP4502D6 metabolism of several TCAs as well as many commonly prescribed medical drugs (such as quinidine), thereby raising the blood levels of these medications and producing serious side effects. Zoloft (sertraline) also inhibits the CP4502D6 enzyme, but less potently than Prozac or Paxil.

Luvox (fluvoxamine) inhibits the CP4501A2 isoenzyme, which metabolizes the neuroleptic drug Clozaril (clozapine; see Chapter 7), the Alzheimer's disease drug Cognex (tacrine; see Chapter 6), the asthma drug Bronkaid (theophylline), as well as caffeine and nicotine. Luvox, like Prozac, also inhibits 3A4 and can raise blood levels of all of these substances to produce unwanted side effects (see Table 2.13).

Celexa (citalopram) does not inhibit cytochrome enzymes.

Since older patients commonly take more than one medication, it is useful to keep in mind the potential for drug interactions that may be caused by SSRI antidepressants. These interactions are shown in the Appendix, Tables A.2 and A.3, pages 139–167.

TABLE 2.13. Medications Whose Effects May Be Increased by 3A4 Enzyme Inhibition

---

- Antibiotics
  Pediazole (erythromycin)
  Achromycin (tetracycline)

- Halcion (triazolam)

- Haldol (haloperidol)

- Hormones (replacement estrogen and progesterone)

- Hismanal (astemizole)

- Lanoxin (digoxin)

- Seldane (terfenadine)

- Steroids

- Xanax (alprazolam)

MISCELLANEOUS ANTIDEPRESSANTS

Some newly developed antidepressants have diverse chemical properties and do not neatly fit into existing medication categories. Like SSRIs, these antidepressants are effective for treating severe as well as mild to moderate depression, although some doctors prefer to use them only if the older depressed patient has not responded to other antidepressants, or has experienced side effects. Each, however, has been effective when all other antidepressants have failed. Drugs in this category are Wellbutrin (bupropion), Effexor (venlafaxine), Serzone (nefazodone), and Remeron (mirtazapine).

Wellbutrin (bupropion)

Wellbutrin possesses a number of properties that are advantageous for the older patient. It is not sedating, does not cause decrease in blood pressure, and has no anticholinergic properties. Its broad dosing range,

37.5–125 mg/day, allows for great flexibility in selecting an optimum dose. Because Wellbutrin increases physical energy, it can be taken in the morning by older people who feel overly sedated or lack enough energy or motivation to get started in the day.

The main disadvantage of Wellbutrin for older patients is the agitation and insomnia that can develop with treatment. It also has to be taken more than once per day, although a new preparation called Wellbutrin SR (sustained release) is now available for once-per-day dosing. Experience with this new sustained-release preparation in older patients is limited. Wellbutrin has no effect on the heart, so a pretreatment EKG is not necessary. Since it also does not alter the function of liver isoenzymes, there are no alterations of blood levels of other antidepressants.

The starting dose of Wellbutrin is 37.5–75 mg and the average daily dose is 150–225 mg. The starting dose of Wellbutrin SR is 75 mg in the morning, and the daily dose is 150–300 mg.

Effexor (venlafaxine)

Effexor shares many of the pharmacological and therapeutic properties of TCAs, but lacks anticholinergic side effects, making it particularly useful for older depressed patients. Effexor has a very broad range of effective doses, from 12.5–300 mg/day. Like Wellbutrin, it also has to be given more than once per day, although a new sustained-release preparation (Effexor XR) permits a single daily dose. Common Effexor side effects are nausea, vomiting, and headache. Effexor also raises blood pressure, which may diminish its usefulness for some older patients. Very low doses, such as 12.5 mg (one-half of a 25-mg pill) or 18.75 mg (one-fourth of a 75-mg pill) often eliminate or markedly reduce the severity of these side effects. It appears that the extended-release form of Effexor (Effexor XR) produces less severe side effects than the original drug. Nevertheless, starting with low doses and very gradually increasing the dose only when the patient is not experiencing side effects is probably prudent clinical practice. Most older patients will achieve therapeutic response at doses between 75 and 100 mg/day.

Serzone (nefazodone)

Serzone has a broad therapeutic dose range, allowing for great flexibility in selecting the correct dose. Its relatively sedating effect often induces a restful night's sleep early in the course of treatment. As treatment progresses, however, the dose may have to be decreased as unwanted daytime sedation develops. Serzone does not cause orthostatic hypotension or anticholinergic side effects.

Like SSRIs, Serzone may interfere with CP450 enzymes that metabolize other medications, thereby increasing their blood level and potential side effects. In particular, Serzone strongly inhibits the 3A4 isoenzyme family. Medications metabolized by CP4503A4 whose effects may be increased by the simultaneous use of Serzone are shown in Table 2.13 on page 51.

Remeron (mirtazapine)

Remeron is a relatively new antidepressant. Although clearly effective in younger and middle-aged adults, research and clinical experience is not as extensive in older individuals as other antidepressants. Nevertheless, Remeron may be useful for the older depressed individual, since it does not cause anticholinergic or cardiac side effects, or orthostatic hypotension. It is very sedating, however, and causes moderate weight gain. Older patients who still drive an automobile should be warned of this sedation, and overweight elderly people should avoid taking Remeron.

MONOAMINE OXIDASE INHIBITORS (MAOIs)

MAOIs are the oldest of the antidepressants, first discovered (like many psychiatric drugs, by accident) in the 1950s and widely used throughout the world since. MAOIs deplete the important presynaptic enzyme monoamine oxidase, which metabolizes norepinephrine and serotonin throughout the body and in the brain. The enzyme inhibition treats depression by increasing synaptic levels of norepinephrine and serotonin in the central nervous system.

MAOIs are excellent antidepressants for some older patients, sometimes effective when all other antidepressants have failed, and especially helpful for the older depressed person who is listless and apathetic. Two MAOIs are available for use in the United States, Nardil (phenelzine), and Parnate (tranylcypromine). There is little significant difference between these drugs in either therapeutic benefit or side effects. However, as with all antidepressants, some older patients will respond more favorably to one than the other.

As with the TCAs, basic guidelines for MAOI use include a careful medical evaluation, tests of thyroid function, and an EKG. A measurement of blood pressure, seated and standing, is also advisable, since these drugs may lower blood pressure. Most importantly, the prescribing physician must be informed of every medication, over-the-counter drug, vitamin, mineral supplement, or herbal preparation that the patient is taking, since some medications, or other substances with stimulant properties, and the pain medication Demerol (meperidine) interact with MAOI antidepressants with potentially serious results.

The basic principles of treatment of older patients with MAOIs follow those of the other antidepressants. *Starting doses should be low, and dosage increases made gradually.* Once an effective therapeutic dose is reached, the older person must stay on the medication for a sufficient period (2 to 3 months) to develop the full therapeutic effect. Prolonged maintenance treatment with MAOIs follows the same course as for tricyclics and SSRI antidepressants: Older individuals who have had repeated serious depressive episodes over the course of their life may need to stay on MAOIs indefinitely, although doses usually decrease over time. Starting doses and therapeutic doses of the MAOIs are shown in Table 2.14.

TABLE 2.14. MAOI Antidepressants

Drug	Starting dose	Therapeutic dose
Nardil (phenelzine)	7.5–15 mg/day	15–45 mg/day
Parnate (tranylcypromine)	5–10 mg/day	10–40 mg/day

Side effects of MAOIs include potentially serious orthostatic hypotension, with a likelihood of unsteadiness and falling if the older person stands up too quickly. Some older patients are sedated by MAOIs (especially Nardil); others may be stimulated and made somewhat more anxious or agitated (especially by Parnate). MAOIs occasionally increase blood pressure and should not be given to patients with hypertension.

Despite their efficacy, MAOIs possess a number of characteristics that make them difficult for the average elderly person to use. Apart from side effects, these include restrictions on some commonly eaten foods and other medications that may be taken along with the MAOIs due to their interaction with the medications or chemicals present in the food (see Table 2.15). These interactions cause blood pressure to rise, resulting in a severe pounding or throbbing headache in the back of the skull that is not relieved by aspirin. In more serious cases, the rise in blood pressure may lead to a potentially fatal stroke or even heart attack.

The medications that older patients commonly take that may interact with MAOIs to cause a rise in blood pressure are shown in the Appendix, Table A.2, pages 139–144.

Elevations in blood pressure also occur when tyramine-containing foods interact with an MAOI. Tyramine in significant amounts is found in aged, aromatic, cheeses, as well as pickled meats, fishes, and vegetables. The cheese with the highest tyramine content is cheddar, but all aged "smelly" (and often delicious) cheeses have sufficient

TABLE 2.15. Foods Containing Tyramine That May Increase Blood Pressure When Interacting with MAOI Antidepressants

• Cheese (cheddar, parmesan, mozzarella, and any aged, aromatic cheeses) • Aged, aromatic cheeses • Parmesan, mozzarella • Pickled meats (e.g., sausages, paté)	• Pickled fishes (herring, salmon, paté) • Fava beans • Avocados • Chocolate (in large amounts) • Aged chianti wine

tyramine to interact with an MAOI, as do cheeses in Italian and Mexican foods. The older patient who is taking an MAOI must *never* eat aged cheese or pickled Italian or Mexican foods.

Dietary restrictions should not make an elderly patient fearful of taking an MAOI antidepressant. Following these dietary and medication restrictions usually prevents hypertension while taking MAOIs, although headaches occasionally develop when a food containing cheese is unwittingly eaten, for example, when dining out. It is important, therefore, to inquire about the ingredients of any foods or sauces that may be served away from home. Foods that must not be eaten while taking MAOI antidepressants are presented in Table 2.15 on page 55.

Older patients, their families, and prescribing physicians need to be warned that a patient who develops a serious headache while taking an MAOI must be taken to an emergency room immediately. The administration of Regitine (phentolamine) or Procardia (nifedipine) will immediately lower the blood pressure, stop the headache, and prevent a stroke or heart attack.

MAOIs are best used for older patients who are still reasonably physically healthy, are not taking other medications, can still prepare their own foods, and who are capable of administering their own medications. Otherwise, a caretaker must supervise administration of the MAOI, ensure adherence to the dietary restrictions, and be alerted to the possibility of unfavorable drug reactions with other medications.

STIMULANTS

Psychomotor stimulants such as Ritalin (methylphenidate) have been used for many years to treat elderly patients who are apathetic and withdrawn but not otherwise depressed. Doses of Ritalin, 2.5 mg up to 20 mg/day, can be remarkably effective even in very elderly patients, have few side effects, and do not cause cardiotoxicity, although mild tachycardia may occur. Amphetamines and other stimulant drugs, also effective, are less commonly used to treat older patients.

Ritalin, prescribed alone as an antidepressant, often increases agitation and can significantly interfere with sleep. For this reason, it is recommended in doses of 2.5–5 mg/day to augment the therapeutic effect of other antidepressants.

Ritalin is most effective taken in the morning and early afternoon (e.g., at breakfast and at lunch), since doses taken any later may interfere with sleep.

ELECTROCONVULSIVE THERAPY (ECT)

ECT has been in use as an antidepressant treatment since 1938. For the first 25 years of its use, however, it was a treatment that often produced serious side effects. Since the 1960s, research and clinical experience have helped both physicians and patients understand the benefits as well as risks of this treatment. Modern ECT, a medically sophisticated treatment with well-described standards and procedures, is safe and painless.

ECT is the most effective treatment of serious late-life depression, especially for those whose serious depression also includes delusions and delusional depression (see page 27). It is especially helpful for the old or very old, frail elderly patient whose life may be at risk because of severe depressive symptoms.

Before treatments begin, patients must undergo a comprehensive physical examination, laboratory tests, EKG, and sometimes X rays. ECT is usually given in the morning, and the patient must not have anything to eat or drink (including medications) after midnight the previous night. Treatment usually takes place in a specially equipped room, after an anesthesiologist administers a short-acting anesthetic, atropine, and a skeletal muscle relaxant. A brief modified seizure lasting between 10 and 30 seconds is produced by an electrical current. Oxygen is provided before and during the treatment as well as in the posttreatment period. The patient usually then awakens slightly dazed and confused for another 2 to 5 minutes. Most patients, even very old patients, rapidly recover from this confusional state and are able to eat breakfast and return to their rooms within a half-hour. There are almost no immediate side effects except for occasional headaches.

A single or a few ECT treatments are usually not sufficient to treat a severely depressed older patient, especially if delusions are present. Four to six treatments are generally necessary, and occasionally 12 or more, given every other day. Delusions often disappear quite rapidly, leaving the patient somewhat bewildered or even amused when asked about them ("I never thought such a thing"). However, along with improvement, comes mild, short-term memory loss for recent events before and during the period of treatment. Although the memory loss is usually not more serious than this brief impairment, for reasons still unknown, an occasional older patient will experience more extensive memory loss.

Other side effects or risks of ECT are minimal, assuming the older patient is in good physical health. Virtually all older patients except those with brain tumors can be treated with ECT. Even older patients who have had a prior heart attack can be safely treated with ECT provided they have recovered sufficiently. Despite the need for hospitalization, general anesthesia, and the experience of a brief seizure, the therapeutic benefits of ECT for the severely depressed older patient far outweigh the memory impairment also caused by the treatment.

Unlike antidepressant treatment, ECT is not continued after the depression lifts. Rather, relapse is prevented by prescribing an antidepressant or a combination of antidepressant and mood stabilizer such as lithium for patients who have recovered. Occasionally, elderly patients who have suffered the most severe depressions and have received many drug and ECT treatments may need follow-up treatments with ECT if the posttreatment medication is not helpful.

BIPOLAR DEPRESSION

Some depressions alternate with states of elated mood, irritability, and excessive activity. Previously called manic–depressive disorder, the diagnostic term "bipolar" disorder (discussed in Chapter 3) is now applied.

An older patient rarely develops bipolar disorder for the first time, although it is quite common for bipolar disorder to continue into late life, often becoming more severe unless it has been adequately treated. It is important to determine whether a depression is part of a bipolar pattern. Depression associated with bipolar illness may gradually or suddenly switch into a manic state of increased energy, elation, or irritability (more commonly in the elderly). *Antidepressant medication accelerates this switch.* A history of prior manias will alert the physician to the need for careful dosing to avoid inducing such a switch. Should the older person not know or have forgotten previous manic episodes, the family can be of great assistance in providing this information. Indicators that suggest a prior manic episode are listed in Table 2.16.

Bipolar disorder in the elderly is a serious illness. Late-life depression that is part of a bipolar pattern is treated with the same antidepressant drugs used to treat all other forms of late-life depression. Because of a possible switch into mania, however, physicians usually prescribe extremely low starting doses (even lower than usual for old people), or combine antidepressants with mood-stabilizing drugs to prevent the switch. Whether or not treatment with a mood stabilizer hastens a switch to depression cannot be determined with certainty, but it is not unusual to see an older person become depressed soon after beginning a mood stabilizer at doses traditionally used with younger patients. The following case illustrates the diagnostic and treatment complexities of an elderly depressed man with bipolar illness.

THE CASE OF MR. I: BIPOLAR DEPRESSION

A 78-year-old retired, first-rate accountant, Mr. I was referred to a psychiatrist because he was having difficulty sleeping. At the time of the first interview, he bounded into the psychiatrist's office

TABLE 2.16. Indicators of a Prior Bipolar Episode

• A period of unusual exuberance
• A period of loud and rapid talking that is difficult to interrupt
• A period of irresponsible money spending
• A period of notable decrease in need for sleep
• A period of unusually increased interest in sex
• A period of elation, euphoria, or grandiosity
• A period of irritability and unusually short-tempered behavior

grinning from ear to ear, with sparkling blue eyes and a ruddy complexion. He grasped the hand of the psychiatrist and offered his gratitude for the appointment. This well-dressed man sat alert and upright in his chair. He spoke rapidly but appropriately, occasionally making a small joke or commenting on a cartoon that he had seen. It was quite apparent that Mr. Y was in a state of hypomania of many weeks' duration. In reviewing his history, it was also clear that he had had numerous episodes of hypomania and his energy and enthusiasm had been the source of his considerable professional success. He was loved by his friends, who relied upon him absolutely for his organizational talents and mathematical abilities. He spoke of enjoying life, but of needing one or two drinks in the late afternoon to calm down, and then having great difficulty sleeping, often awakening in the middle of the night despite the use of an over-the-counter sleeping medication.

Mania in older people is exhibited more as irritation than as euphoria. Mr. I was somewhat unusual in his buoyancy and joviality. Indeed, he was so pleasant to be with that it seemed almost absurd to label him as having a disorder of mood regulation. However, his attempts to stabilize his mood in the late afternoon illustrate the risk that some elderly hypomanic patients take by using excessive alcohol to calm themselves or to help them sleep. A combination of alcohol and over-the-counter sleeping pills, or sleeping pills that are prescribed by a primary care physician who does not recognize the hypomania, can lead to disorganized thinking, impaired judgment, and even psychosis.

Since Mr. I had mild kidney problems, lithium, customarily used to treat mania, was not considered a suitable treatment. He was started on a mood stabilizer and within 2 weeks he was calmer and sleeping longer hours. He again expressed his deep gratitude to the psychiatrist and promised to stay in touch.

Two weeks later, Mr. I called the office, sounding like a different person. His voice was now very slow and barely audible. He said he felt terrible about bothering the psychiatrist, since there was really no point in making contact. When he arrived for the appointment, he was obviously profoundly depressed. No longer well groomed with sparkling eyes and rosy cheeks, he sat slumped in his chair, sighed frequently, and asked imploringly, "What's the point?" Although not suicidal, he repeatedly commented that he would not mind if he did not awaken the next morning.

Since Mr. I was already on a mood stabilizer, an antidepressant was started despite the risk of a switch into mania. However, Mr. I's depression did not improve, and he was unable to work or socialize. His appetite vanished, he began to lose weight, and he looked progressively more haggard at each visit. At one interview, he mentioned to the clinician that he had been writing thank-you letters to all of his friends. Although he denied being suicidal, the clinician correctly recognized this behavior as the forerunner to an impending suicide attempt and hospitalized Mr. I. In the hospital, Mr. I was found to have psychotic thinking and was treated with ECT. After 1 week, Mr. I was again chatting with all the patients, leading a discussion group in the evening, and flirting with the nurses. When visited by the doctor, his sparkling eyes and ruddy complexion restored, he boomed, "Thanks, Doc, I feel great again!"

Trying to balance hypomania and depression in an elderly person requires considerable finesse and a willingness to use doses that are considerably lower than commonly used with younger and middle-aged adults. Even so, older patients with bipolar disorder may exhibit markedly labile moods, switching rapidly from mania to depression and back following a manipulation of medication, a change in dose, or a discontinuation. This was certainly true of Mr. I.

THE ROLE OF PSYCHOTHERAPY

Depending on the severity of an older person's depression, psychotherapy may or may not be useful. For mildly or moderately depressed states, psychotherapy together with antidepressant treatment may effectively help an older individual with losses that are common in late life, as well as with painful earlier life experiences that have weighed heavily over the years. A recent research study found that the combination of psychotherapy and antidepressant medication was superior to either treatment given alone to elderly patients (Reynolds, Miller, Pasternak, et al., 1999). Older individuals are often excellent psychotherapy patients, and therapeutic work with them can be gratifying. Characteristics that suggest the usefulness of psychotherapy in an older person include the following:

- Sufficient physical energy to come to appointments
- Sufficient mental energy to engage in a dialogue
- Absence of dementia
- Awareness of being depressed

Some older patients, however, may be too severely ill to benefit from psychotherapy until their depression has been at least partially, if not entirely, resolved. Those who lack the motivation or physical or mental energy to come to regular appointments and discuss their emotional state will not benefit from psychotherapy. The presence of dementia or delusions, or other forms of psychotic thinking, usually indicate that an older individual is not a candidate for psychotherapeutic treatment.

Most caregivers and clinicians who work with older people probably engage in a form of psychotherapy, whether or not they are consciously doing so. Concern, empathy, and supportive listening can be quite therapeutic in themselves. It is important neither to patronize older persons nor minimize their degree of suffering from depression. Openly talking about losses, suicidal thoughts, and past failures can be very comforting when such discussions take place in an atmosphere of mutual trust and acceptance, and many clinicians have discovered that older depressed individuals make wonderful psychotherapy patients. They are often willing to be more honest about their emotions and to take responsibility for their own past failures or disappointments; they readily form therapeutic relationships (even with younger therapists) that can sustain them during the early phases of their treatment with antidepressant medication.

Depressions that are serious enough to require medical or psychiatric attention, however, should not be treated with psychotherapy alone. Milder depressions can rapidly deteriorate, while serious depressions, if not actually life threatening, certainly impair quality of life.

Chapter 3

MANIA

Mania is a state of increased excitement, energy, and activity accompanied by decreased sleep, impulsiveness, rapid thought, and speech. In young adults, manic states are usually associated with a euphoric, elated mood in which the individual feels excessively overconfident and even grandiose, bestowed with special powers, vision, and understanding. These states of mania (or the less pronounced hypomania) can be brief or prolonged, alternating with normal mood states (euthymia) or, more typically, with depression. Mania alternates with depressive states that may also be of short or long duration, mild or severe, and even life threatening. In most cases, the depression is characterized by a profound loss of energy, motivation, and interest (see Chapter 2). This alternation of mania and depression is known as bipolar disorder.

Development of mania for the first time in late life is relatively unusual. Elderly people who become manic display irritability (dysphoric mania), elation, or mania mixed with depression. If they have not been fully manic as younger adults, they will have experienced periods of increased energy. Consequently, clinicians should carefully question family members as well as the patient about unusually energetic states in earlier years. Historical diagnostic indicators of mania are shown in Table 3.1 on page 64.

A great deal is known about the course of bipolar disorder in relation to the aging process. As with many recurrent illnesses, bipolar disorder tends to become more severe as the individual ages, and the severity of each mood state, whether high or low, tends to in-

TABLE 3.1. Characteristics in Young and Middle-Aged Years That Are Indicators of Mania in Old Age

- Prior diagnosis of mania as a young adult
- Presence of mania in a relative, especially parent or grandparent
- Periods of unusually high energy as a young adult
- Lifelong states of high energy
- Lifelong need for less sleep than average
- History of periods of impulsive spending
- History of periods of impulsive sexual behavior

crease over time. Thus, hyperactive states that were quite enjoyable and productive in young adulthood can become so severe in old age that they trigger psychotic thinking and irrational, impulsive behavior. Similarly, depressive states considered normal perturbations of everyday mood in younger years can become profound and even life threatening in late life. Characteristics of late-life mania are shown in Table 3.2.

Not only do high and low mood states become more severe with approaching old age, but the alternation between high and low may become more rapid, with less time spent in normal euthymic states; this is known as "rapid cycling." Rapid cycling bipolar disorder is defined as four or more complete cycles (e.g., high to low to high, or low to high to low) in any 12-month period. Many patients begin to show a pattern of rapid cycling as they become elderly, contrasting with the manic or depressed episodes of longer duration when they were younger. Some very severely affected elderly individuals are always in either a manic or a depressed state without any intervening period of normal mood stability.

In late life, the characteristics of a manic or hypomanic episode begin to change, so that the clinical presentation of an elderly manic patient is different from that of a young or middle-aged patient, and even different from the way the individual may have appeared when younger. While euphoric mania does occur, in general, older manic

**TABLE 3.2. Characteristics of Elderly
Patients with Bipolar Disorder**

- Increased energy
- Restlessness
- Decreased sleep
- Intrusiveness
- Impulsive spending
- Inappropriate sexual behavior
- Unusual or inappropriate irritability
- Unusual outbursts of anger, criticism
- Depressed as well as elated moods
- Rapid shifts in mood
- Paranoid or unusually suspicious thinking

patients are more irritable and angry, and less elated and euphoric. These dysphoric manic elderly patients are intrusive, highly irritable, explosively angry, and disagreeable. They are often irrationally argumentative and extremely critical. Moreover, it is not unusual for elderly dysphoric manic individuals to exhibit paranoia, characterized by an unusual degree of suspiciousness, or even to develop delusional beliefs that others intend to inflict harm. Dysphoric paranoid mania is illustrated in the following case vignette.

THE CASE OF MR. J: MANIC PARANOIA

Mr. J, a distinguished and well-dressed 80-year-old gentleman, sat fidgeting in the doctor's office. He insisted that he had only come to the appointment at the behest of his children, who had become a nuisance to him. "They are constantly pestering me and watching over me," he barked at the doctor, adding "I think they just want my money. There is really nothing wrong with me; I'm finally having a good time in my life."

Now retired, Mr. J had been an extremely successful business executive who had indeed become wealthy. He had always been unusually energetic and, as a younger man, seemed to need little sleep. Consequently, he was able to work long into the evening hours, which contributed to his business success. His children described him as a man who had an unusually strong temper, but he could also be the life of the party at family gatherings or social events, where he would become uncharacteristically loud, flirtatious, and boastful of his unusual abilities. At times, Mr. J could be obnoxious, but more typically, he was very funny, with a seemingly endless repertoire of jokes. As he grew older, however, his good moods began to vanish. He was aware of his growing irritability, which he attributed to business stress.

Mr. J's children decided on a psychiatric evaluation after several episodes in which he had telephoned town officials complaining of neighbors' behavior. He had also made numerous calls to his attorney, questioning the provisions of his will, then announcing that he might have to change attorneys and rewrite his will because of a conspiracy between his children and his legal advisor to deprive him of his fortune. Family gatherings were now characterized by constant bickering or even violent arguments about nearly every subject. Mr. J was unable to remain seated at a dinner table, and when not quarreling, he would get up and pace around the house. He interrupted other peoples' conversations and became inappropriately critical of his young grandchildren, whom he had previously adored.

During the consultation, Mr. J revealed that he slept only a few hours a night and was usually awake by four in the morning. He was restless throughout much of the day and had difficulty concentrating when he tried to read or watch television. At first, he described his mood as normal, but as the evaluation progressed, he admitted to being both angry and unhappy.

The mixture of despondency, elation, grandiosity, and increased energy is termed **mixed mania** and is especially characteristic of elderly people who have a rapid cycling, dysphoric manic presentation. These individuals often laugh and cry either simultaneously or in rapid alternation. And, like other elderly bipolar patients, they are unusually irritable and have explosive tempers.

THE RANGE OF MANIC AND HYPOMANIC BEHAVIOR IN LATE LIFE

Not all manic behavior in older people is destructive or requires treatment. For some older individuals, extra enthusiasm is part of their delightful personalities and helps them continue to function well into very late life. Only when they are frustrated or criticized can their mania turn irritable, nasty, and aggressive. Nevertheless, it is important for clinicians to recognize these less serious manic states because of their potential for intensifying and interfering with life. The following case vignettes illustrate the shift from delightful enthusiastic hypomania to impulsive and irritable behavior that occasioned concern among family members.

THE CASE OF MRS. K: MANIC ELATION

Mrs. K was a vivacious 76-year-old with a twinkle in her eye and a bright smile. "I love life," she announced to the doctor during her first interview. Indeed, she was unusually athletic and still an accomplished skier, tennis player, hiker, and kayaker—activities that brought her great pleasure. Still employed part-time, she was writing a book and was a devoted grandmother in her large and close-knit family.

Mrs. K's enthusiastic and delightful behavior actually masked a slowly emerging manic state. The first diagnostic indication was an increasing predilection for shopping at yard sales. In the weeks prior to her first interview, Mrs. K had impulsively purchased a number of expensive items, none of which she or any of her children needed. When questioned about these purchases, she brightly announced that she would be able to sell the items at a profit, and expressed surprise at the family's concern. As it transpired, the items were not easily disposed of, but since Mrs. K had become an inveterate shopper at yard sales, neither she nor her children considered these impulsive purchases to be a sign of anything wrong.

Later that week, Mrs. K was involved in a minor automobile accident. Ordinarily an extremely accomplished driver, Mrs. K drove into oncoming traffic without looking. She was greatly chagrined and embarrassed when her car was hit broadside, and she recalled wondering whether she was developing Alzheimer's disease. Apart from a failure in concentration, there were no other signs that Mrs. K was developing Alzheimer's disease or had a memory impairment.

A second accident prompted Mrs. K to seek a psychiatric evaluation. As she drove her car from the body repair shop where the first accident damage had been repaired, she was again hit by an automobile. (The owners of the body shop were astonished to see her return with more damage 5 minutes after she had paid the bill and driven away.) Once again, the accident had been the result of a failure of attention and concentration on Mrs. K's part.

In the diagnostic interview, Mrs. K admitted that she had been sleeping less, and while awake at night, cleaned her basement and organized her papers. "I thought it was wonderful that I had so much energy," she commented. However, she also revealed that she had been having more arguments with friends, and that her children's behavior seemed to annoy her more than usual. On reflection, she conceded that her concentration was no longer what it had once been. She had great difficulty reading a newspaper through, and she was considerably more restless than usual.

When the doctor inquired about instances of unusual energy or high spirits in other members of the family, the diagnostic picture became clearer. Mrs. K's father and grandmother had both displayed unusual energy and impulsive behavior. Two of Mrs. K's children had experienced periods of elation, and one had suffered from a manic episode that required medical attention. When Mrs. K further revealed that as a young adult she had suffered from at least one serious depression that had required treatment, her behavior was unequivocally diagnosed as manic.

Patients like Mrs. K require diagnostic sleuthing on the part of a clinician. However, with careful questioning, the pattern of late-life mania preceded by earlier examples of bipolar mood shifts in both patient and family helps point the way to an accurate diagnosis. A comparable pattern was true of Professor L.

THE CASE OF PROFESSOR L: MANIA AND CREATIVITY

Professor L, known as impossible to get along with, was world-renowned in his field. He was irritable, had a roaring bad temper, and managed to alienate almost everyone with whom he worked. At age 50, he sought medical attention because he was unable to sleep and his thoughts were racing out of control. He was diagnosed as having mania and placed on lithium.

For the next 22 years, Professor L's behavior was "normal." No longer irritable or objectionable, his colleagues, friends, and family now enjoyed his company. His sleep was normal, and his work productive. It appeared that treatment with lithium had eliminated his manic illness.

But Professor L was not content. He told the doctor, "I am no longer a genius. My work is excellent and perhaps outstanding, but it is not creative." Without his mania, Professor L's work, although still far above average, was no longer original. He insisted on stopping his lithium.

Several months after he had stopped taking lithium, Professor L, now age 73, again went to see his doctor. He reported that his friends were shunning him and that he was unusually short-tempered. Everybody suddenly seemed "stupider and slower" to him. However, his mind was flooded with ingenious ideas, although none of them had been particularly effective. From his perspective, his "genius" had returned; from everyone else's perspective, so had his mania.

Mania is not eradicated by medication even though the symptoms may be controlled. Patients who have been manic frequently wish to stop their medication because they miss the "high" symptoms. It is also not unusual for patients who are well-controlled with mood-stabilizing drugs to believe that their illness has ended, and that the mania will never return even when they discontinue medications. When medication is discontinued, however, the illness invariably reappears, at times even more severe than before treatment. Research data indicate that the relapse rate when medication is discontinued is very high, especially among individuals who have suffered from bipolar illness for many years, as in the case of the elderly (Baldessarini, Tondo, Suppes, et al, 1996). Despite medication side effects or the loss of the "high," elderly patients who have been manic but are now well-stabilized should be encouraged to continue their medication.

Sometimes it is possible to maintain an elderly individual on low doses of mood-stabilizing medication in a hypomanic state that is otherwise well-stabilized and free from depression. Mrs. M was one such person.

THE CASE OF MRS. M: ACCEPTABLE HYPOMANIA

Mrs. M went to see a psychiatrist at age 65. She was profoundly depressed and had been depressed many times in the course of her life. In between periods of depression, however, she was a delightful, bubbly woman whose behavior was not unusual. When first treated with antidepressant medication as a younger woman she became hypomanic. In this state, she was inappropriately flirtatious, spent an enormous amount of money impulsively and quickly, and became unusually critical of her husband, with whom she enjoyed a close relationship.

Each subsequent episode of depression was treated with antidepressants, and each treatment produced a manic state that, while enjoyable for Mrs. M, was unacceptable to her husband and family. She commented, "I don't see what everybody was worried about—I felt great." But her manic behavior was indeed unacceptable. She would take sudden long trips without telling anyone where she was going; she would stop strangers on the street and harangue or flirt with them; her behavior in stores led to her being asked to leave several times; her house became increasingly disorganized and her charge card bills rose enormously.

After many attempts at finding the right balance in medication, her doctor finally arrived at the optimum combination: extremely low doses of an antidepressant medication together with a mood stabilizer. Her mood remained mildly elevated; she was bright, talkative, and flirtatious. But neither her family nor her husband found this behavior unpleasant or worrisome. Their greatest concern was the large telephone bills that accrued from frequent calls to her friends, children, and grandchildren scattered throughout the United States. This aside, however, her behavior was delightful and acceptable, and as far as Mrs. M and her husband and family were concerned, additional therapeutic treatment was not necessary.

Finding an appropriate dose of medication that is acceptable to the patient and family can be difficult, but it is a critical goal of treatment. Once a stable medication regimen is established, the patient should remain on this treatment program as long as possible.

TREATMENT OF MANIA

At this point in time, treatment of manic states in young and middle-aged adults using lithium carbonate or anticonvulsant agents as mood stabilizers is well established. For elderly patients who are suffering from mild to moderate manic symptoms, a mood-stabilizing medication can be given alone, and, after approximately 2 to 4 weeks of treatment, the mania usually begins to subside. Unfortunately, many elderly patients who have had lifelong bipolar disorder develop progressively severe symptoms that cannot be maintained on mood-stabilizing medications alone. For these patients, particularly those who are agitated, sleepless, or psychotic, neuroleptic medications are combined with mood stabilizers and the patient is maintained on both for at least 3 to 6 months. Since many of these patients also have frequent depressive episodes, an antidepressant drug is often added to the mood stabilizer/neuroleptic combination, and the doses of the three drugs are balanced to minimize all the symptoms without producing excessive side effects. After a period of stability, which varies from patient to patient (usually 12 symptom-free months), the neuroleptic is usually very gradually tapered and discontinued. This practice of using combinations of drugs according to the severity of mania in older patients does not differ substantially from treatment in young and middle-aged adults. The starting dose of mood stabilizers is usually lower for elderly patients than for younger patients, and maintenance doses may also be lower. The mood stabilizers and their doses for older patients are listed in Table 3.3 on page 72.

Neuroleptic drugs that are used to help control mania are the same as those discussed in Chapter 7. In general, nonsedating medications are preferred because excessive sedation may cause the following problems in elderly patients:

- Impaired ability to participate in daytime activities
- Diminished nighttime sleep
- Orthostatic hypotension

TABLE 3.3. Mood-Stabilizing Medications

Name of drug	Starting dose	Maintenance dose	Therapeutic blood level
Lithium	300–600 mg/day	600–900 mg/day	0.2–0.6 meq/ml
Depakote (valproate)	125–250 mg/day	600–1,200 mg/ day	35–75 ng/ml
Tegretol (carbamazepine)	100–200 mg/day	300–600 mg/day	4–10 ng/ml
Lamictal (lamotrigine)[a]	12.5–25 mg/day	[b]	—
Neurontin (gabapentin)[a]	300–600 mg/day	[b]	—

[a]Therapeutic dose not determined for elderly patients.
[b]Maintenance doses not determined for elderly patients.

For these reasons, typical neuroleptics such as Haldol (haloperidol) and Prolixin (fluphenazine), or the atypical neuroleptic drugs Risperdal (risperidone), Zyprexa (olanzapine), and Seroquel (quetiapine) are used alone or in conjunction with mood stabilizers. Clozaril (clozapine), also a very effective treatment for mania, causes considerable side effects in the elderly and should be prescribed only by physicians experienced in its use. The doses of neuroleptics for the treatment of mania are shown in Table 3.4.

Use of Mood Stabilizers in the Elderly

Lithium

Elderly patients tend to be more sensitive to the effects of lithium than young and middle-aged adults. Because of this increased sensitivity, it is especially important to evaluate carefully the older patient's state of medical health before embarking on a course of lithium therapy. The components of this evaluation are listed in Table 3.5.

Lithium treatment is initiated using a very low first dose (150–

TABLE 3.4. Neuroleptics Used to Treat Mania

Name of drug	Therapeutic dose
Clozaril (clozapine)	10–100 mg/day
Haldol (haloperidol)	0.25–3 mg/day
Prolixin (fluphenazine)	0.25–3 mg/day
Risperdal (risperidone)	0.25–3 mg/day
Seroquel (quetiapine)	25–100 mg/day
Zyprexa (olanzapine)	0.5–5 mg/day

300 mg), which is then gradually increased to between 600 and 1200 mg/day (two or three pills a day). After 1 week, the lithium plasma level should be checked. Plasma levels as low as 0.2 are sometimes effective, but during the acute manic state, higher blood levels may be necessary to produce a full therapeutic response. For more intensive treatment, the dose is gradually increased until the blood level reaches

TABLE 3.5. Pretreatment Lithium Evaluation

Diagnostic test	Reasons for test
1. Complete blood count	1. Lithium increases white blood cell count.
2. Kidney function (serum creatinine; urinalysis)	2. Lithium impairs renal excretion and causes increased thirst and urination.
3. Weight	3. Lithium may cause weight gain.
4. Electrocardiogram	4. Lithium alters cardiac conduction.
5. Thyroid function tests (T_3, T_4, TSH)	5. Lithium causes hypothyroid states.

0.5 or 0.6 meq/liter or until side effects begin to appear. The dose and blood level are then held constant for approximately 1 week and then rechecked. The dose can be raised or lowered depending on the patient's clinical condition and the appearance of side effects.

In older patients, a variety of side effects may develop at relatively low doses. Alerting the patient and family to the possibility of these early side effects and the need to report them will help with dosage adjustments. The most serious of these early effects are a subtle confusion, memory loss, and disorientation. These symptoms of cognitive impairment, frequently present in very old people, are easily mistaken as the natural signs of the aging process rather than as lithium side effects. Other side effects that are common early responses to lithium include nausea, diarrhea, and bloating. Typically, the individual who takes lithium is also thirstier, drinks more fluids, and urinates more frequently. An increased need to urinate at night may significantly disrupt sleep, so that the dose of lithium and its corresponding blood level need to be reduced.

Once a patient's manic symptoms begin to diminish, there should be no further increases in lithium dosage. Now, the task is to ensure that the patient continues to take this effective dose in order to sustain mood stability and prevent recurrence. It is not always easy to maintain an elderly person on lithium because of side effects, and frequent office visits or telephone check-ins can improve compliance. Plasma concentrations should be checked every 3 months, as should the complete blood count. Tests of renal (serum creatinine, urinalysis), heart, and thyroid function should be conducted every 6 months.

A variety of commonly used medications may impair renal clearance of lithium by older individuals. These include thiazide diuretics, nonsteroidal antiinflammatory drugs, and certain antibiotics (such as tetracycline). In each case, lithium blood levels will increase, causing more side effects.

Lithium can be safely given with neuroleptics, however, and, as already noted, this combination effectively controls severe symptoms of manic patients regardless of age. Although an occasional patient may become more confused when lithium and a neuroleptic are taken together, low doses of each are almost always safe and should be considered state-of-the-art psychopharmacology for the treatment of the seriously ill manic elderly patient.

Depakote

Depakote (valproate; also called divalproax sodium or Depakene) is an anticonvulsant drug that also stabilizes mood. The principles of prescribing Depakote are the same as for lithium. A pretreatment medical evaluation and tests of liver function (SGOT, SGPT, AST, alkaline phosphatase, BUN) are necessary, although thyroid function does not have to be assessed. As with lithium, the starting doses of Depakote are kept low (125–250 mg), and each subsequent dosage increment is small. Dosage changes are based on the therapeutic effects of the previous dose and on the appearance of side effects. As with lithium, the goal is to find a dose that is effective but produces only minimal side effects, if any, and then to maintain the older individual at this dose (and plasma level). Therapeutic Depakote plasma levels (50–100 ng/ml) should be checked weekly until the patient's mood has stabilized and thereafter every 3 to 6 months; liver function tests should be checked every 6 months.

Since side effects of Depakote tend to be milder than those of lithium and do not involve the kidneys, there is no increased thirst or urination. High doses of Depakote may cause weight gain, but at the usual low doses given to older patients, weight gain, if present at all, tends to be minimal. Some older patients become somewhat more confused and forgetful when taking Depakote. This, too, partly depends on dose and blood level. At very low doses, these side effects should not be significant.

Elderly patients with rapid cycling bipolar disorder generally do not respond well to lithium. Although Depakote, usually in conjunction with a neuroleptic, is commonly used, these older patients may need substantial doses of medication in order to become stabilized, and balancing the need for a stable mood against the debilitation of serious side effects is difficult. Even with medication, these patients may oscillate between mania, depression, and drug toxicity. Mrs. N's condition illustrates this dilemma.

THE CASE OF MRS. N: PROGRESSIVE BIPOLAR DETERIORATION

Mrs. N, an 80-year-old woman, had a serious bipolar disorder that first appeared at age 20. Both her mother and grandmother also had experienced bipolar disorder and a number of siblings were either depressed or manic. As a young woman, Mrs. N had responded well to lithium treatment, although she had gradually gained weight. By age 40, however, she was experiencing frequent depressions that depleted her of energy and made it impossible for her to function at work. In between depressions, she would have brief periods of normal mood, then experience a period of greatly increased energy. At these times, she would fight with her husband, shout at her children, and alienate her friends. Attempts to control the progressive nature of her illness with neuroleptic medications were only partially successful because she developed side effects to these medications as well.

By age 60, Mrs. N was essentially nonfunctional; she was unable to work and care for her home or family. Both depression and mania were now characterized by psychotic thinking: Mrs. N believed that the police, neighbors, and her family intended her harm. Depakote and lithium were combined with a neuroleptic, which helped stabilize her mood and decrease her psychotic thinking, but when she took therapeutically effective doses, she experienced considerable difficulty concentrating and remembering.

By age 80, Mrs. N was either hospitalized or in a nursing home all the time. She now appeared severely demented: disoriented, forgetful, and unable to read or concentrate on a television program. Her moods were brittle and shifted rapidly during the course of an hour. Attempts at controlling her moods with medication almost always failed due to serious side effects. At this stage, the only treatment helpful to Mrs. N was to provide comfort and safety.

Tegretol

Tegretol (carbamazepine), like lithium, is an anticonvulsant that also stabilizes the moods of bipolar patients. It was the first anticonvulsant recognized to have this effect and is still used widely for young and middle-aged adults, although information on its use in the elderly is limited.

Pretreatment medical evaluation for Tegretol includes measuring the white blood cell count, since Tegretol can occasionally cause agranulocytosis. Unlike Depakote, treatment with Tegretol is not associated with weight gain, but, like the other mood-stabilizing medications, it can impair concentration and memory. Starting doses of Tegretol for the elderly are usually 100–200 mg/day, with dosage increments of 100 mg/day up to 600 mg, or to the point where mood has been stabilized. Plasma levels of Tegretol (8–12 ng/ml), like Depakote, correlate with the therapeutic response and can help guide the clinician.

Once an older manic patient's mood has stabilized, Tegretol treatment is continued in the same manner as that of lithium or Depakote, with duration depending on the severity of the patient's symptoms, frequency of prior manic episodes, and the appearance of side effects. In general, elderly patients have had many prior episodes of mania, so that clinicians tend to maintain Tegretol treatment indefinitely provided that serious side effects do not develop.

Tegretol is unique among the mood stabilizers in accelerating the liver metabolism of certain drugs, and it therefore may *decrease* the blood levels of itself, necessitating occasional dose increases as well as other therapeutic medications. Drugs whose blood levels may be lowered by Tegretol are listed in the Appendix, Tables A.2 and A.3, pages 139–167.

Neurontin

Neurontin (gabapentin) is a relatively new medication used in the treatment of bipolar disorder. Like Depakote and Tegretol, it is an anticonvulsant, but recent experience suggests that it may also be effective in controlling mania in some young and middle-aged patients. There are no research studies comparing its therapeutic effectiveness with lithium, Depakote, or Tegretol, and there are no research studies on its effectiveness in the elderly. However, it is a promising drug for older patients with bipolar disorder because it does not interact with other medications and has very few side effects.

The effective range of Neurontin doses for young and middle-aged adults is between 900 and 3,000 mg/day. Lower doses may be effective for some elderly patients, but it is possible that others will require the full therapeutic dose. Regardless of which dosage will ultimately be necessary to control mania in an older patient, the starting dose should be low (300–600 mg/day), so that the prescribing clinician can judge the effect of the drug without producing side effects.

The only significant side effect of Neurontin is sedation, and taking it at bedtime may help an older manic individual sleep. During the day, Neurontin may be used to calm older manic patients who are agitated, restless, or impulsive. However, excessively sedating an older person may interfere with nighttime sleep and thus inhibit participation in other therapeutic activities.

Neurontin does not have any significant interactions with other medications. It can be combined safely with lithium, Depakote, or Tegretol for elderly patients with mania whose behavior is severely out of control, and with antidepressants for patients with bipolar disorder and rapid mood oscillation. It can also be combined with medications given to treat other medical illnesses.

Lamictal

Lamictal (lamotrigine), another anticonvulsant, is also a relatively new medication used for psychopharmacological purposes. In young and middle-aged adults, it has mood-stabilizing properties and may even have a modest antidepressant effect. Unfortunately, because of side effects, Lamictal must be used carefully and doses increased very slowly. If high doses are given too rapidly, a serious rash may develop and progress to Stevens–Johnson syndrome.

Since the efficacy of Lamictal in the elderly has not been well studied and has the potential for causing a serious rash, trials in controlling late-life manic episodes with this drug are limited. Should a clinician wish to prescribe Lamictal, it is important that starting doses should be very low (e.g., 12.5–25 mg), and each small dosage increment made no more frequently than once a week. The therapeutic dose range for Lamictal in the elderly has not been established. For young and middle-aged adults, the usual suggested range is 100–300 mg/day. This is likely to be too high for the elderly, and 25–75 mg will probably be as effective. Lamictal cannot be given in conjunction with Depakote because of an adverse drug interaction.

Another relatively new anticonvulsant, Topamax (topiramate), is being used with increased frequency to stabilize mood in younger patients. At present, there is no reported experience with this medication in the elderly.

Maintenance Treatment

Regardless of the mood-stabilizing drug that is selected, maintenance medication is almost always necessary. Since older patients with mania are likely to have had numerous prior manic and depressed episodes over the course of their lives, they are at great risk for relapsing into yet another manic or depressive phase. In order to prevent relapse, clinicians should continue treating older patients with the dose of mood stabilizer that has been therapeutic. In order to ensure that side effects do not develop or worsen over time, it is necessary to evaluate the patient every 3 to 6 months, depending on mood stability and the appearance of side effects.

There are times when it becomes necessary to reduce the dose of a mood stabilizer or to discontinue it entirely, especially when serious side effects or drug interactions have occurred. Recent studies of lithium discontinuation in younger adults have found that rapid or abrupt discontinuation almost always results in relapse into a manic or depressed episode (Baldessarini, Tondo, Faedda, et al., 1996). The more rapidly the lithium is discontinued, the more likely the relapse. Although these studies have focused almost entirely on lithium treatment of younger patients, there is no reason to believe that older patients taking other mood-stabilizing medication will respond differently to drug discontinuation. Therefore, in order to avoid relapse in the elderly, all mood-stabilizing medications should be gradually discontinued.

Chapter 4

ANXIETY

There are many reasons to become anxious as one ages. Loss of health and financial independence, as well as the death of friends and loved ones, are normal and common causes of anxiety. Although symptoms of anxiety, like those of depression, are often encountered in older people, anxiety disorders are relatively uncommon in late life (less than 4%). Anxiety is intensified by the presence of illness, infirmity, and apprehension regarding assisted living, nursing home placement, or hospitalization, and is exacerbated by interrupted sleep, excessive caffeine and alcohol, and cigarette smoking. To compound the problem, some of the commonly used medications given to treat late-life illnesses may worsen anxiety.

DIAGNOSING ANXIETY

Anxiety is the clinical term for extreme worry that becomes preoccupying and interferes with normal functioning and quality of life. Most older people, like their younger counterparts, experience anxiety as an inner sense of tension, apprehension, or dread of the future. Physical symptoms usually include headaches, sighing, pressure in the chest, difficulty swallowing, heart palpitation, and a variety of minor gastrointestinal discomforts including excess gas, constipation, and frequent bowel movements. Anxious people often have trouble falling asleep, either eat too much (often sweets or junk food) or lose their appetite, startle easily, and are irritable. Extreme anxiety is evident in an apprehensive facial expression with furrowed brows and pursed lips, shaky legs, jittery hands, and a general sense of restlessness.

Anxious older people sometimes become unreasonably preoccupied with their health, making frequent contacts with, or visits to, physicians. Fears of developing cancer, an imagined impending heart attack, or simply worrying about a variety of shifting aches and pains that accompany old age become greatly magnified and further intensify the subjective experience of anxiety. Because anxiety also interferes with concentration and memory, it is quite common for anxious older people, who are already more than normally forgetful, to begin to imagine that they are developing Alzheimer's disease.

Anxiety Disorders

When the symptoms of anxiety persist over a period of weeks and interfere with normal functioning, the diagnostic term **generalized anxiety disorder** is applied. Four other discrete clusters of symptoms have anxiety as their basis and are also considered to be anxiety disorders: phobias, posttraumatic stress disorder, panic attacks, and obsessive–compulsive disorder. **Phobia** is the term applied to a collection of unreasonable but often common fears such as fear of snakes, heights, and enclosed spaces. Older people do not have more phobias than younger people, although they are often fearful, with reason, of being alone or of leaving home alone. Worries about falling or having an accident in the street, being mugged, or getting lost in unfamiliar places commonly prevent old people from leaving home but do not necessarily constitute a phobia. This particular anxiety is generally more common among older people living in inner cities with relatively meager financial resources and few friends or family.

Posttraumatic stress disorder (PTSD) is the term given to a variable group of symptoms including anxiety, interrupted sleep, startle reactions, and flashbacks to a traumatic event. Palpitation, perspiration, headache, and extreme apprehension are also symptoms of this disorder. There are no clinical studies on the prevalence and diagnostic criteria, or on the treatment of PTSD in the elderly.

Panic attacks are sudden sensations of extreme apprehension or terror. Typically, a person experiencing a panic attack fears loss of control, dying (usually from a heart attack), or going insane. Extreme physical symptoms of gasping for air, chest pain, and profuse sweating become overwhelming to the degree that most people, young or old, seek medical help, often in a hospital emergency room. The following case illustrates a recurrence of panic attacks initially believed to be late-life depression.

THE CASE OF MR. O: DEPRESSION MASKING PANIC

A 75-year-old man was brought to a psychiatrist by his son, who said that his father was extremely depressed. Mr. O acknowledged feeling sad, fidgeted in his chair, sighed frequently, and offered few spontaneous thoughts or questions.

In the course of the consultation, his son mentioned in passing that Mr. O had suffered frequent panic attacks since serving in the infantry during World War II. Despite the length of time that had elapsed since the war, he continued to be unusually nervous in crowds and avoided them whenever possible. At times, he would suddenly feel as though he could not breathe and feared he was having a heart attack. This was exacerbated by heart bypass surgery he had undergone 10 years earlier, even though he was fully recovered and nonsymptomatic. In recent years, he had become more reclusive, rarely venturing from his home. He stopped driving because he was afraid that "something would happen" to him while driving.

Mr. O was placed on an antidepressant. He responded well and has remained on this medication with significant benefit, free of both depression and panic attacks.

It is unusual for panic attacks to appear for the first time in old age (Salzman & Sheikh, 1998), and Mr. O's history is typical of the older person whose panic attacks began in young or midadulthood. These continue into old age and, commonly occurring together with depression, worsen in frequency and intensity.

Obsessive–compulsive disorder is another condition compounded by significant anxiety that appears in early life and worsens with age. Symptoms include excessive rumination about irrational or unrealistic scenarios as well as persistent thoughts of unworthiness, guilt, or anger: "Why did I do it?" or "What did that person mean?"; "If only I had. . . . " Over and over, the person is plagued by a compelling, often frightening image, such as jumping in front of a car or stabbing an acquaintance. Sometimes repetitive thinking is accompanied by behavior that cannot be resisted: Excessive hand-washing, repeated checking of door locks and stoves, and avoiding cracks in the sidewalk are common examples. Compulsions are not more frequent in late life, but the symptoms can be crippling. In the following case, a retired lawyer was beset by the obsessive worry that her life was a failure.

THE CASE OF MRS. P: OBSESSIVE RUMINATIONS

Mrs. P had been known throughout the United States as a distinguished and successful lawyer whose opinions were frequently sought, and whose writings were regularly used in teaching law students. Despite these outward signs of considerable success, reinforced by the high esteem of colleagues, friends, and students, she had experienced periods of great self-doubt, usually under the stress of a deadline. At these times, she would begin to worry that she had "fooled everybody" and was not nearly as successful as everyone believed. Over and over again, she would review her many professional decisions and erroneously discount many of them as incorrect. She had trouble falling asleep and would sometimes awaken early in the morning, ruminating about what she termed "a life that was not all it could have been." In daytime meetings or while waiting for a red light to turn green, she would find her mind filled with doubts and even a sense of shame and guilt. She would perspire, fidget, and feel disconcerted. As a young and middle-aged woman, these periods of uncertainty and self-recrimination lasted only hours or occasionally days. Following retirement at age 70, however, she noticed that she had become more ruminative and more unsure as the years passed.

Mrs. P did not lack for activities in her retirement. She had writing projects and continued a voluminous correspondence. She still served as a consultant, and some of her research was coming to fruition. Nevertheless, she found herself once again doubtful about her abilities and her past successes. Her anxious ruminations began to interfere with her ability to concentrate. She denied feeling depressed and stated that her energy, sleep, and appetite were all fine. She still enjoyed an active sexual relationship with her husband of many years but fretted almost continuously about her inability to become absorbed in her work.

Psychotherapy and low doses of an SSRI antidepressant in combination with a benzodiazepine afforded Mrs. P significant diminution of her symptoms. After 1 month at the same dose, she reported feeling less troubled than she had for many years.

Anxiety in late life is almost always accompanied by depression, the two occurring together so often that some authorities consider them to be symptoms of the same disorder. Because the treatment required for each may differ, it is useful for physicians to distinguish between anxiety and depression. Table 4.1 lists some of the indicators that differentiate the two in late life. The following clinical case exemplifies the interplay between symptoms of anxiety and depression in the elderly.

TABLE 4.1. Differentiating Symptoms of Anxiety and Depression

Category of symptom	Anxiety	Depression
Expression	Alert, worried, tense	Listless, apathetic, withdrawn
Bearing	On edge, nervous, fidgety	Slumped, few movements, dejected, frequent sighing
Attitude	Apprehensive; "The sky is falling in."	"What's the use?"
Sleep	Trouble falling asleep	Trouble staying asleep
Energy	Not usually affected	Markedly diminished
Thoughts	"There must be some help for me."	"Nothing will help—it's hopeless."
The future	Uncertain	"There is no future."

THE CASE OF MRS. Q: ANXIETY DISORDER
WITH DEPRESSIVE SYMPTOMS

Mrs. Q, a frail 86-year-old woman, arrived at her doctor's appointment shuffling slowly and wearing a shapeless house dress and ill-fitting wig. She had a pleasant smile but looked very worried, often pausing and stuttering as she recounted her story. Widowed for many years, Mrs. Q lived alone and was still able to manage her own cooking, cleaning, and home maintenance. She had very few pleasures in life and seemed in low spirits, but she did not have disturbed sleep or impaired appetite and denied feeling hopeless or persistently despondent. Rather, she worried continually, any news item that she saw on television or read in the newspaper causing her to fret. She seemed oblivious to her appearance and state of health but continually brooded about the health of family members and friends. She sighed frequently, shifted uncomfortably in her chair, and played with the hem of her dress. She constantly excused herself and apologized for being a bother.

The physician decided to treat Mrs. Q for anxiety with medication. He carefully instructed her not to take more than the usual dose and explained that she might become dependent. His warning that the medication might cause her to become more forgetful elicited the response, "Oh, I'm already so forgetful it couldn't get worse." He further cautioned her about the possibility of falling, a common side effect of benzodiazepines in the elderly, and reminded her to use her walker whenever she stood up. The following week Mrs. Q came to her appointment looking much happier and more relaxed. She stuttered less frequently and no longer fidgeted with the hem of her dress.

Although feeling anxious from time to time is common in old age, it may be caused or exacerbated by medications or be a response to, or part of, a physical illness. Medications taken by the elderly that commonly cause or increase anxiety are shown in Table 4.2 on page 86.

Medical illnesses often associated with excessive anxiety or that may increase anxiety in the elderly are shown in Table 4.3 on page 86.

TABLE 4.2. Medications That Cause or Increase Anxiety

- Stimulants (including caffeine)
- Thyroid hormone
- Steroids
- Cough medicines containing ephedrine-like compounds
- L-Dopa or other dopaminergic agents

TREATMENT OF ANXIETY WITH BENZODIAZEPINES

Although different types of medications, especially antidepressants, are increasingly used to treat anxiety, benzodiazepines are still most commonly prescribed to anxious patients of all ages. Despite side effects that may occur in older patients, benzodiazepines are remarkably safe and effective for anxiety as well as for insomnia (discussed in Chapter 5).

TABLE 4.3. Medical Illnesses That Cause or Increase Anxiety

- Hyperthyroidism
- Heart failure
- Chronic obstructive pulmonary disease
- Excessive adrenal gland function
- Hypoglycemia
- Pheochromocytoma
- Small stroke

Surveys indicate that approximately 40% of all benzodiazepine prescriptions are written for elderly people (Salzman, 1998). At least one-third of older people in nursing homes take benzodiazepines, and this number may rise to almost 50% among those who are seriously ill (Salem-Schatz & Fields, 1992). In many circumstances, they are probably overprescribed or inappropriately prescribed.

Broadly speaking, benzodiazepines can be divided into two categories based on their elimination half-life, which determines how rapidly they are cleared from the body. The first group, having a long half-life, are slowly excreted. During the aging process, excretion becomes even slower, causing these long half-life medications to accumulate gradually in the bloodstream. In the second group, the short half-life compounds, metabolism is not affected by the aging process, the half-life remains short, and there is no accumulation of medication in the bloodstream. The two categories of benzodiazepines are shown in Table 4.4.

Because they do not accumulate in the bloodstream, current clinical practice strongly favors the use of the short half-life medications in the elderly. Ativan (lorazepam) and Serax (oxazepam), in particular, are used because their doses can be adjusted for older patients quite easily and their effects rapidly clear when the drugs are discontinued. Xanax (alprazolam) has an intermediate half-life and is not recommended as frequently. As a general principle, benzodiazepines with long half-lives are rarely prescribed for the elderly.

TABLE 4.4. Benzodiazepines Categorized by Length of Half-Life

Long half-life	Short half-life
Valium (diazepam): 30–100 hr	Xanax (alprazolam): 12–15 hr
Librium (chlordiazepoxide): 50–100 hr	Ativan (lorazepam): 8–12 hr
Klonopin (clonazepam): 18–50 hr	Serax (oxazepam): 8–12 hr

Prescribing Benzodiazepines for Older Patients

All of the basic principles described in Chapter 2 for treating depression also apply to the treatment of anxiety with benzodiazepines. As sedating drugs, benzodiazepines share therapeutic properties and side effects with other sedative hypnotics, including alcohol. Prior to prescribing a benzodiazepine, it is essential to obtain a complete list of all medications that are being taken by the older patient, especially medications with sedating properties. Nonprescription drugs such as antihistamines and sleeping pills may produce significant daytime sedation when combined with a benzodiazepine. Alcohol, in particular, may also interact with benzodiazepines to increase sedation, unsteadiness, and forgetfulness, and should never exceed the equivalent of one glass of wine. It may be necessary to obtain information from family members regarding excessive alcohol or other sedative use in an older patient.

The basic geriatric prescribing principle of "start low and go slow" applies to the treatment of anxiety with benzodiazepines. Because of age-associated central nervous system changes in neurotransmission and receptor sensitivity, older people are more sensitive to benzodiazepine effects and are sometimes given unnecessarily high doses by well-meaning physicians who do not take this into account. Appropriate starting doses and therapeutic dose ranges of benzodiazepines for the elderly are shown in Table 4.5.

Most benzodiazepines are prescribed to elderly people for a few days or weeks by family practitioners. Short-term benzodiazepine

TABLE 4.5. Starting Doses and Therapeutic Dose Ranges of Benzodiazepines

Medication	Starting dose	Therapeutic dose range
Xanax (alprazolam)	0.125 mg/day	0.125–2 mg/day
Ativan (lorazepam)	0.25 mg/day	0.25–2 mg/day
Serax (oxazepam)	7.5–15 mg/day	15–60 mg/day

treatment can safely and rapidly help control the sudden anxiety brought on by such situations as family crisis or hospitalization.

Long-term use of benzodiazepines for treatment of chronic anxiety lasting weeks, months, or even years is somewhat more controversial because of the development of dependence and the susceptibility of older people to side effects. Surveys of long-term benzodiazepine use in the elderly have found a number of shared symptoms, shown in Table 4.6 (*American Psychiatric Association Task Force Report*, 1990). For these elders, long-term daily benzodiazepine treatment restores quality of life, improves functioning, and helps in the treatment of other illnesses. Many old people who take benzodiazepines for a long period of time find that these medications are effective and safe, especially when doses are kept low (Pinsker & Suljaga-Petchel, 1984). When elderly patients need to take a benzodiazepine for a prolonged period of time, or even indefinitely, clinicians should carefully monitor dose and side effects, taking into account that the aging process increases sensitivity to all benzodiazepine effects.

Side Effects of Benzodiazepines

Except for the possibility of increased sedation when taken with other sedating drugs, benzodiazepines are extremely safe medications for older patients. There are virtually no drug interactions with the exception of Xanax (alprazolam), whose metabolism is impeded by the anti-

---

TABLE 4.6. Symptoms Common to Older Individuals Requiring Long-Term Benzodiazepine Treatment

- Chronic anxiety mixed with chronic depressive symptoms
- One or more serious medical illnesses
- Chronic pain (such as arthritis)
- Chronic heart disease
- Social withdrawal because of anxiety or panic disorder

depressant Serzone (nefazodone), causing a significant rise in Xanax's blood level. This interaction results in excessive sedation, falls, and cognitive impairment. Benzodiazepines are also suitable for older patients because they do not cause anticholinergic side effects or orthostatic hypotension. Common benzodiazepine side effects are shown in Table 4.7.

Sedation

Sedation commonly caused by benzodiazepine use in the elderly increases the danger of becoming involved in an automobile accident, especially when the benzodiazepine has a long half-life (Barbone et al., 1998). It is essential, therefore, to caution older individuals about the sedating effects of benzodiazepines and the consequence of impaired driving ability. Sedation also decreases attention, memory, concentration, and motivation in the elderly.

Unsteadiness

In low doses, benzodiazepines rarely cause significant unsteadiness. As doses increase, however, muscular coordination and agility decrease, resulting in unsteadiness when standing up and walking. An elder who is already unsteady and who uses a cane or walker for assistance may find that higher doses of benzodiazepines further impair balance.

TABLE 4.7. Common Benzodiazepine Side Effects

- Sedation
- Unsteadiness
- Falls
- Forgetfulness
- Withdrawal reactions

Falls

An increased propensity for falling has been reported with both long and short half-life benzodiazepines (Ray, Griffin, & Downey, 1989). Older patients should therefore be warned about this potential side effect and be advised to stand up slowly and walk carefully when taking a drug from this class.

Forgetfulness

Benzodiazepines may cause forgetfulness in older people and also further an already present memory loss. For this reason, some clinicians are reluctant to treat anxious elderly individuals with benzodiazepines. The degree of memory impairment caused by a benzodiazepine is, however, rarely significantly disabling and is limited to very recent events. It is directly correlated with dose—the higher the dose, the worse the memory impairment—and disappears when the medication is discontinued. Moreover, since anxiety itself interferes with memory, reducing anxiety with low doses of a benzodiazepine may actually improve memory. If a benzodiazepine is prescribed during an acutely stressful situation, the dose should be kept low and the drug should be discontinued as soon as possible. Benzodiazepines should not be given to elderly patients with seriously failing memory, especially those with Alzheimer's disease.

Depression

Despite occasional published case reports, benzodiazepines do not initiate depression in depression-prone individuals (Smith & Salzman, 1991), and they do not exacerbate depressive symptoms. On the contrary, benzodiazepines are often extremely helpful in treating older individuals who are both depressed and anxious.

Dependence on Benzodiazepines

Physiological dependence develops when a benzodiazepine is taken on a regular basis for more than a few weeks, and a mild withdrawal reaction may occur if the drug is abruptly stopped. Most patients do not become dependent for at least 2 months, and dependence is correlative with dose: The higher the dose, the shorter the period of time before dependence develops.

Significant dependence develops over a longer treatment period, causing a variety of typical withdrawal symptoms that appear when the drug is suddenly discontinued. In order to minimize these, benzodiazepines should always be gradually discontinued over a few days or weeks. The longer a benzodiazepine has been taken (years, for example), the longer the tapering period should be (several weeks). Benzodiazepine withdrawal symptoms are shown in Table 4.8.

Long-term treatment of anxiety with benzodiazepines does not cause older individuals gradually to increase the dose in order to satisfy drug craving, and clinical experience and research data indicate that elderly individuals who take benzodiazepines on a long-term basis actually show a tendency to decrease their dosage over time (*American Psychiatric Association Task Force Report*, 1990).

THE CASE OF MR. R: SUCCESSFUL, INTERMITTENT BENZODIAZEPINE USE

Mr. R was a retired, 71-year-old accountant who had suffered from anxiety his entire life. Constantly worried about illness, he often imagined that he had a serious or even fatal disease. Anxiety about contracting an illness in a foreign country kept him from

TABLE 4.8. Benzodiazepine Withdrawal Symptoms

- Sudden increase in anxiety
- Sudden worsening of sleep
- Restlessness, agitation
- Unsteadiness
- Flu-like symptoms
- Seizures (after very high doses)

traveling away from home. At work, he worried about his accomplishments and was overly sensitive to what he interpreted as criticism from his coworkers. Mr. R had nevertheless lived a productive and successful life. He was married, the father of two, with two grandchildren. At the time he sought treatment, he was in excellent physical health, although he regularly woke early in the morning feeling severely anxious and apprehensive about the coming day and continued to feel mildly on edge throughout much of the day.

Physical examination failed to reveal any significant disorder that might be causing his anxiety or jitteriness. He did not smoke, drink, or excessively drink coffee or tea. He exercised regularly and maintained a balanced diet.

A benzodiazepine was started with excellent response. He rapidly felt less anxious and nervous, his hypochondriasis diminished, and his sleep improved.

Fearing dependence, Mr. R tapered and discontinued the benzodiazepine approximately 6 months into treatment. He remained symptom-free for 2 years, after which he began experiencing heart palpitations. When blockage of one coronary artery was discovered and angioplasty was recommended, he became acutely anxious. His face took on a fixed worried stare, his muscles became chronically tense, and he could neither sleep nor sit still. He sighed, sweated, could not concentrate, and became convinced that he was about to die. The benzodiazepine was restarted, with rapid relief of symptoms. Following a successful angioplasty, Mr. R again discontinued the benzodiazepine. He now leads a vigorous and happy life, free from anxiety, confident that a benzodiazepine can provide an anxiolytic "safety net" during times of extreme stress.

Mr. R's case illustrates the recurrent nature of anxiety commonly seen in the elderly. Symptoms of anxiety interfere with quality of life, worsen illness, and disrupt sleep, and pharmacological treatment is warranted when their cause can be neither determined nor removed. Like Mr. R, many anxious elderly do not experience anxiety for long periods and are able to remain drug-free unless a stressful circumstance revives symptoms.

TREATMENT OF ANXIETY
WITH OTHER MEDICATIONS

Almost any medication that has mild sedating properties will help decrease anxiety. Antihistamines or aspirin, for example, are commonly taken by older people for mild anxiety. Buspar (buspirone) is a prescription medication sometimes used as an alternative to benzodiazepines. It is considerably less sedating, does not cause memory impairment or dependence, or anticholinergic side effects or orthostatic hypotension (Hart, Colenda, & Hamer, 1991). The usual starting dose is 10 mg, one to three times per day, and the effective daily dose range is 10–80 mg/day. However, it may take from several days to more than a week for therapeutic effect to begin, whereas the anxiolytic effect of benzodiazepines is experienced within a half-hour to an hour.

Beta blockers constitute another class of drugs that is sometimes helpful for the treatment of anxiety. Commonly used to treat heart disorders or high blood pressure, these drugs are frequently effective in reducing physical symptoms of anxiety such as tension, nervousness, and sighing. However, because these drugs affect the heart and blood pressure, older people with heart disease, high blood pressure, or arrhythmias should not be prescribed a beta blocker unless their family physician or cardiologist approves its use.

Recently, several antidepressants have been approved by the U.S. Food and Drug Administration for treatment of anxiety disorders in young adults. There are no research data describing the use of antidepressants (Effexor for general anxiety; Paxil for social anxiety disorder), but clinical experience suggests that any antidepressant with sedating properties may be useful as a treatment for anxiety.

Chapter 5

SLEEP DISORDERS

Difficulty falling asleep and staying asleep, awakening too early in the morning, and overall lack of restorative, restful sleep are probably the most common complaints of older people. It is important to determine the cause of disrupted sleep—whether it is due to the natural aging process or to a treatable condition—before embarking on a course of treatment.

THE EFFECT OF AGING ON NORMAL SLEEP PATTERNS

As people grow older, changes in the normal pattern of sleep are predictable. Some of these are due, in part, to an age-related alteration in monoamine neurotransmission, as well as to a decrease in melatonin, the primary hormone that regulates normal sleep cycles. During the course of a night, more time is spent in bed but less of this time is actually spent asleep. It becomes increasingly difficult to fall asleep (especially among women), and sleep is frequently interrupted by brief awakenings that become more common in the early morning hours. By 4:00 or 5:00 A.M., many older individuals are fully awake or only able to doze intermittently thereafter. They consequently feel tired throughout the day and need a daytime nap. Research studies indicate that four out of five older people find a short nap during the day helpful (Cardakson, Brown, & Dement, 1982). However, prolonged daytime naps generally cause subsequent disrupted nighttime sleep and should be avoided.

CAUSES OF DISTURBED SLEEP

In addition to age-associated sleep disruption, several other factors that further compound the problem are shown in Table 5.1.

Pain and trouble breathing are common and often overlooked causes of disturbed sleep. For example, simply changing position in bed can cause sufficient pain to awaken an older arthritis sufferer. Similarly, breathing complications increase with age in both men and women. Sleep apnea, characterized by excessive snoring, gasping, and periods in which the sleeper seems not to breathe at all (apnea), is frequently encountered and, besides interrupting sleep, may present a threat to health. Five or fewer apnea episodes per hour are usual in approximately three-fourths of older men and one-third of older women, and do not constitute a disorder (Gillin & Ancoli-Israel, 1998). When apnea episodes occur more than 10 times per hour, however, sleep is disrupted to the degree that most older people are significantly fatigued the following day. Because a sleep apnea syndrome requires medical treatment, caretakers and clinicians who work with the elderly should always inquire about serious snoring, especially when the older person complains of daytime drowsiness. Benzodiazepines, antipsychotic medications, alcohol, or sleeping pills may aggravate sleep apnea.

Depression and anxiety are also primary causes of sleep disturbance in the elderly when not adequately treated. Daytime drowsi-

TABLE 5.1. Common Causes of Disturbed Sleep in the Elderly

• Physical
  Pain
  Sleep apnea
  Muscle twitches
 	
• Emotional
  Depression
  Anxiety
	• Substance use
	  Alcohol
	  Tobacco
	  Caffeine
	  Medication
	
	• Circumstantial
	  Noisy bed partner
	  Noisy neighborhood
	  Outside noise

ness and fatigue due to poor sleep can become debilitating, exacerbating unsteadiness and forgetfulness, and contributing to spiraling anxiety and depression. In younger adults, anxiety impedes falling asleep (initial insomnia), whereas depression causes early morning awakening (late insomnia). This differentiation does not apply to older patients who routinely experience difficulties both falling and staying asleep, as they ruminate over their problems. The degree to which anxiety and depression disrupt sleep in the elderly is underappreciated, and when other possible precipitants have been eliminated, the clinician should look for symptoms of depression and anxiety.

Alcohol, caffeine, and nicotine generally interfere with sleep in people of all ages. Even if only taken as the morning cup of coffee or tea, caffeine's stimulant effects can last from 12 to 20 hours. Smokers experience lighter sleep than nonsmokers, while even a small amount of alcohol at suppertime can induce wakefulness in the middle of the night. Although alcohol's strong sedating properties help generate sleep, its rapid metabolism can cause abrupt awakening several hours later.

A number of medications including beta blockers; stimulating drugs such as Ritalin (methylphenidate) and nonprescription nasal decongestants and appetite suppressants; hormones; and drugs used to treat asthma and cardiac arrhythmias can fragment sleep, with subsequent daytime drowsiness.

Severe sleep difficulties encountered in an older person may be due to normal, age-related changes in sleep patterns being compounded by a lifelong a pattern of disordered sleep. This will almost invariably result in fear of not falling asleep each night, as illustrated by the case of Mr. S.

THE CASE OF MR. S: LIFELONG PATTERN OF SLEEP DIFFICULTIES

Mr. S had had trouble falling asleep since childhood. As a teenager, he could only sleep in his own bed and was unable to attend summer camp or sleep at friends' homes. At college, he slept fitfully in his dormitory room and would return home on weekends to sleep in his own bed.

When Mr. S married, he found it difficult to sleep in the same bed with his wife. He tossed and turned, awakening frequently and sometimes even crying out. After several years of this tortured nighttime routine, she suggested that he sleep in a separate room, which he did for the remainder of their married life.

In his own room and bed, Mr. S's sleep improved but was never as restful as in his own childhood bed. By the time he was 60, Mr. S worried constantly about whether he would be able to sleep each night. This distress so preoccupied him during the day that he spent his time reading books on sleep and visiting doctors, psychiatrists, and neurologists. He underwent several sleep studies, all of which indicated normal sleep patterns.

At age 70, Mr. S was not only constantly worried about his inability to sleep but he was also depressed. Antidepressant medication improved his mood but tended to further interrupt his sleep, and he discontinued it after a few months.

Five more years found Mr. S awakening between four and five o'clock every morning, no longer depressed, but unable to fall to sleep. These were sometimes happy and productive hours spent exercising, reading, or paying bills. More commonly, however, he lay in bed ruminating over his lifelong sleep disturbance and despairing of ever improving. He argued with himself about whether to take a sleeping pill, which he knew would help him sleep, but which would make him feel guilty for having to rely on a medication. Reluctant to visit hotels or rented vacation houses, Mr. S's life was substantially constricted by his sleep worries, which worsened with age.

Mr. S entered psychotherapy and this, combined with regular use of a benzodiazepine, helped him accept his need for sleep medication without feeling guilty. As his childhood fears were discussed in therapy sessions, his dependence on nightly benzodiazepines gradually decreased, although at times of unusual stress he still found it necessary to take a sleeping pill for a complete night's sleep.

FACILITATING UNINTERRUPTED SLEEP

Sleep hygiene— the term applied to guidelines for restful sleep— requires eliminating any substance, circumstance, or condition that interferes with sleep, and maximizing those factors that promote it, shown in Tables 5.2 and 5.3.

TABLE 5.2. Advice to Older Patients for Eliminating Causes of Disrupted Sleep

- Eliminate caffeine.

- Eliminate cigarettes.

- Eliminate or greatly decrease alcohol use, especially at night.

- Separate from a noisy bed partner (unfortunate, but helpful).

- Seek adequate medical attention for pain, trouble breathing, muscle twitching, sleep apnea.

- Seek adequate medical attention for anxiety and/or depression.

- Seek medical advice about discontinuing or lowering the dose of any medications that interfere with restful sleep.

Even with good sleep hygiene, other methods of inducing sleep may be necessary. Recent research has reported that cognitive-behavioral therapy (CBT) is effective in improving the sleep of older adults (Edinger, Hoelscher, & Marsh, 1992). Sleeping pills, the more obvious agent, should only be used after consultation with a physician.

The elderly use sleeping pills significantly more often than younger adults, accounting for 35–40% of the use of sedative–hypnotic medication in the United States. Nearly one-third of elderly patients take prescription medications for sleep, and the majority of seniors in

TABLE 5.3. Guidelines to Older Patients for Promoting Restful Sleep

- Ensure good nutrition by adhering to a balanced diet.

- Engage in some form of daily exercise.

- Do not read or watch television in bed.

- Limit daytime naps.

- Practice meditation or other self-relaxing techniques.

long-term care facilities regularly receive sedative–hypnotics (Balter & Uhlenhuth, 1992). More than 1 in 10 Americans between the ages of 65 and 69 use over-the-counter medications to help them sleep (Reynolds, Regestein, Nowell, et al., 1998), although whether these medications are actually effective when used on a regular basis is unclear. Benadryl, for example, probably induces sleepiness more than it produces actual onset of sleep.

Antidepressants

When depression is the primary cause of disrupted sleep, prescription of sedating antidepressants can be extremely helpful, as described in Chapter 2. Examples of antidepressants with sedating effects are listed in Table 5.4.

Because of growing concern over side effects and dependence produced by chronic benzodiazepine use, clinicians are increasingly prescribing sedating antidepressants rather than benzodiazepines for their sleep-inducing properties. For example, Desyrel (trazodone) has been used as a sleeping pill for more than a decade; 25–50 mg is usually effective, and increased doses over time do not seem to be necessary. Recently, Serzone (nefazodone, 25–50 mg) and Remeron (mirtazapine, 15 mg) have been used successfully for the same purpose. None of these drugs induces a state of dependence, but like benzodiazepines, they may increase the risk of falls when an older person awakens to use the bathroom at night. These three drugs also produce morning sleepiness and hangover, which can be controlled by dose adjustment.

TABLE 5.4. Antidepressants with Sedating Properties

- Pamelor (nortriptyline)
- Paxil (paroxetine)
- Serzone (nefazodone)
- Remeron (mirtazapine)
- Desyrel (trazodone)

Benzodiazepines

Benzodiazepines are the most common group of medications prescribed for the treatment of disturbed sleep—the same medications used to treat anxiety, but taken at bedtime. The prescribing principle of starting with a low dose and gradually increasing to the lowest effective dose also applies to benzodiazepines used as sleeping pills. As with all medications, clinicians must obtain a comprehensive list of all other drugs that are being taken by the older individual before benzodiazepines can be prescribed for sleep, and use of alcohol and caffeine use must be eliminated or minimized. A short or intermediate half-life benzodiazepine is preferred (see Table 5.5) and should only be used on a regular nightly basis for 2 or 3 consecutive weeks. Interrupted use (e.g., 2 to 4 times per week) may be equally effective. At the end of 2 to 3 months' use, dose must be very gradually tapered before the drug is discontinued.

All benzodiazepines produce side effects, regardless of whether they are used to treat sleep disturbances or daytime anxiety. As noted in Chapter 4, sedation, falls, automobile accidents, and memory impairment are an increased risk when older individuals take benzodiazepine hypnotics, and when taken on a regular nightly basis, they usually cause physiological as well as psychological dependence on the medication.

TABLE 5.5. Benzodiazepines with Short or Intermediate Half-Lives and their Effective Dose Ranges Recommended for Sleep

Drug	Dose range
Ativan (lorazepam)	0.125–0.5 mg/day
Xanax (alprazolam)	0.125–0.5 mg/day
Restoril (temazepam)	7.5–30 mg/day
Ambien (zolpidem)[a]	5–20 mg/day
Sonata (zaleplon)[a]	5–10 mg/day

[a] Ambien and Sonata are chemically slightly different from a benzodiazepine, but their effects are virtually the same.

Despite the recommendation that benzodiazepines only be used for a limited period of time for sleep, many elderly people take them on a regular basis for prolonged periods, especially in long-term care facilities. Although it is not clear whether the drugs retain their effectiveness over a long period of time, older individuals often insist that the benzodiazepine is essential for sleep. When clinicians attempt to discuss side effects, including the risk of dependence, as a reason for not continuing to take these medications on a long-term basis, many elders simply respond that they would rather sleep well than worry about either possibility, citing fear of insomnia as the reason.

Even with short-term use, benzodiazepine hypnotics should never be abruptly discontinued, because withdrawal insomnia (known as rebound insomnia) can be so severe as to preclude all sleep. When this happens, the older person invariably insists on restarting the medication, and it is difficult for clinicians and caretakers to resist the request. Repeatedly taking a benzodiazepine to prevent rebound insomnia inevitably leads to long-term use.

One of the dilemmas of long-term benzodiazepine use is increasing sensitivity to side effects as an older individual continues to age. Daytime sedation, falls, and memory impairment may increase in frequency *even if the dose of the hypnotic medication has not been increased.* To make matters worse, as old people become more forgetful, they sometimes awaken at night and, having forgotten that they have already taken a pill to sleep, take another. Thus, their effective daily dose is doubled, with a notable increase in daytime side effects.

Benzodiazepine hypnotics may be helpful for some older patients with serious medical illnesses such as cardiac disease, cancer, or chronic pain conditions, but they aggravate respiratory illnesses as well as sleep apnea and should not be prescribed for older patients with these disorders.

FACILITATING SLEEP IN OLDER PATIENTS WITH DEMENTIA

Treating disrupted sleep in older people with dementia tends to be difficult due to their increased sensitivity to benzodiazepine side effects. Although there is the possibility of paradoxical next-day effects such as anxiety, agitation, and paranoia, benzodiazepines can be helpful in the early stages of the dementia.

Other medications that may help demented persons sleep include sedating antidepressants and neuroleptic drugs that have sedative properties. For example, Mellaril (thioridazine, 10–75 mg) as well as some of the newer neuroleptics such as Seroquel (quetiapine, 25–100 mg) and Zyprexa (olanzapine, 2.5–10 mg) are often effective sedatives when used at very low doses. More extensive discussion of the use of these medications can be found in Chapters 2 and 7.

Other medications with sedating side effects commonly used to facilitate sleep in elderly patients with dementia include Benadryl and chloral hydrate. Both may be helpful for a few nights but tend to lose their effectiveness over time. Benadryl (diphenhydramine) produces anticholinergic side effects that may intensify the patient's confusion, forgetfulness, and agitation. Chloral hydrate may similarly cause paradoxical anxiety and agitation.

FLEXIBLE PRESCRIBING PRACTICES

Regardless of which medication is selected, prescribing a drug to assist sleep requires frequent evaluation of side effects. Because of older patients' increasing sensitivity to drug augmentation over time, clinicians need to remain flexible regarding doses and prescribing practices, so that they can accommodate the changing needs of the patient. This is illustrated by the case of Mr. T, who had used benzodiazepines to help him sleep for most of his adult life.

THE CASE OF MR. T: CAREFUL ACCOMMODATION TO A PATIENT'S NEEDS

Mr. T, an 82-year-old retired business executive, was still intellectually active, maintaining a small office and retaining a small staff to deal with his voluminous correspondence, letters of recommendation, and consultation reports. He was in good physical health, swam daily, and did not smoke or drink alcohol or caffeinated beverages. An enlarged prostate gland caused him to urinate several times each night.

Mr. T had experienced chronic trouble falling asleep throughout his adult life and for the preceding two decades had regularly taken a benzodiazepine. Although he understood the risks of cognitive impairment, he nevertheless maintained that his sleep was more important to him than his memory. At the time of his initial consultation at age 75, he was taking a nightly benzodiazepine and sleeping well, without significant memory impairment.

After age 75, however, his need to urinate began to increase, resulting in more interrupted sleep and causing almost daily drowsiness. A 30-minute nap after lunch allowed him to function during the afternoon, but he almost always had trouble falling asleep at bedtime, even when he was tired.

By age 80, now in an assisted-living facility, Mr. T was awakening three times a night to urinate, the third time usually at four or five in the morning, when he found it impossible to return to sleep. He insisted on additional benzodiazepine for that early morning hour, but to his dismay, the physicians tried various nonbenzodiazepine medications first, without success. Reluctantly, they acceded to his request. The extra dose was effective, and Mr. T reported that he fell asleep without difficulty, awakening refreshed and clearheaded after an additional 3 hours' sleep.

Mr. T's caregivers, however, told a different story. According to them, following the additional dose, he was always extremely confused, forgetful, and irritable in the morning. As he grew progressively unsteady and forgetful, they suspected that he was hiding pills and taking additional doses.

All attempts at lowering Mr. T's benzodiazepine doses, changing the time of administration, or substituting other medications were fruitless, so the physicians created a new prescribing arrangement. At bedtime, the original benzodiazepine dose was cut in half. Mr. T was allowed to have his full 5:00 A.M. dose if he could not fall asleep after urinating, but he was encouraged to try half of that dose first, with the second half available as a backup. The staff administered all nighttime benzodiazepines, and Mr. T was not allowed to keep any additional pills. Although he protested that he was being treated like a child, his physician was firm in issuing orders to the caretaking staff *not* to give him additional pills even if he insisted. The arrangement worked well: Knowing that he had backup medication but no additional pills, Mr. T was able to return to sleep in the early morning and did not suffer from further increases in unsteadiness or memory impairment.

The case of Mr. T illustrates some of the typical problems that can occur when treating the older person with chronic sleep disturbance. There are no simple rules or even guidelines that can be applied invariably to every older individual, so clinicians and caretakers must be prepared to be flexible when designing treatment programs. In Mr. T's case, the staff's willingness to supervise closely his pill taking, and his physician's willingness to see him frequently to adjust the dose, made it possible for him to safely continue his sleep medication. Such frequent contact and treatment flexibility is the hallmark of effective and caring psychopharmacological treatment of older patients.

Chapter 6

DEMENTIA

A decline in memory is inevitable for many, if not most, older people. Difficulty remembering names, even of close acquaintances, is virtually universal as people age, causing much embarrassment and frequently leading an older person to avoid social interactions. Various techniques exist to assist memory including making lists, developing routines, and always placing a particular object in the same place (e.g., putting eyeglasses only on the dresser). Finding comfortable ways of coping with memory loss in social situations is more challenging. Physicians might recommend that the older person simply say, "I'm sorry, I'm not very good at remembering names and I've forgotten yours." The "senior moment" is an equally graceful excuse, as in "Sorry, I'm having a senior moment; I can't remember. . . . "

Many people who experience the growing forgetfulness of old age fear that they are developing Alzheimer's disease. Some may even become convinced of the diagnosis, when, in fact, they are only experiencing normal **age-associated memory impairment** (AAMI), the term given to the normal cognitive decline associated with the aging process.

Dementia, as opposed to AAMI, is the general diagnostic term to convey impairment in memory, concentration, orientation, and logical reasoning (collectively called **cognitive function**) that is not normally associated with growing old. There are many possible etiologies of dementia, including diseases of the brain (such as Alzheimer's disease), cognitive impairment secondary to stroke (previously called

multi-infarct dementia, now termed **vascular dementia**), depression or anxiety disorders, and the secondary effects of drugs and/or alcohol abuse. Alzheimer's disease, a specific disorder of the brain involving the production of abnormal proteins that increasingly impede vital brain functions, is the most common. Although the various types of dementia have subtle differences in symptoms and diagnostic features, there are common patterns of dysfunction, as shown in Table 6.1.

PROGRESSIVE DETERIORATION WITH ALZHEIMER'S DISEASE

Clinicians as well as caregivers can monitor the course of Alzheimer's disease by observing routine daily behaviors. Early in the disorder, the patient becomes more withdrawn, behaves inappropriately in social settings, and displays progressively impaired ability to carry out routine behaviors such as balancing a checkbook, or finding the way home. There is unaccustomed trouble preparing meals, shopping, or ordering from a restaurant menu. Along with these early changes may be a notable failure of short-term memory and the accompanying tendency

TABLE 6.1. Diagnostic Indicators of Dementia

- Increasing confusion about dates, location, time of year
- Marked forgetfulness
- Constant repetition of questions, words, and comments
- Increasing irritability and agitation, especially at night
- Getting lost inside one's home
- Failure to switch off appliances
- Leaving the stove on
- Inappropriate dressing
- Trouble using the bathroom
- Increasing suspiciousness of other people

to repeat questions or statements many times ("When are we going?"; "It's time to go"). Recent events become difficult to recall and the patient may not know the week, month, or season. Anxiety, depression, and irritability appear with increasing frequency as the older person becomes aware of these errors and forgetfulness. Many older people at this early stage learn to deflect questions that display their impairments or cover them with seemingly inappropriate excuses or irrelevant information, a technique known as **confabulation**. Simple tests of memory, such as asking the person to count forwards and backwards, or to remember three objects after 5 minutes, often reveal these deficits, but failures may be rationalized with such statements as "I was never good in math" or "I stopped paying attention to the news."

As the dementia worsens, normal activities become even more difficult: Walking slows; speech becomes infrequent, with little or no facial animation. Orientation is notably impaired and memory deficits are now obvious. At this later stage, behavioral disturbances also become more frequent: Caregivers must now cope with yelling, hitting, and resisting, as well as increased sleep impairment. Soon it becomes difficult for the person to bathe, dress, or use the toilet without help. Speech continues to decline or may be limited to brief stereotyped phrases ("Nice to see you"; "Can't complain") that the person uses regardless of circumstance. Social interaction becomes severely restricted and psychotic thinking may appear in the form of delusions.

In the most severe stages of the illness, behavioral disturbances are frequent and serious, usually requiring medication. There may be constant pacing, verbal outbursts, and physical threats. At this stage of deterioration, patients are terrified of being left alone and may be afraid to bathe. It is at this point that most families need to hire either a full-time caretaker or find a long-term care facility. The following case vignette illustrates the stereotypical "dotty little old lady" with Alzheimer's disease, whose nighttime behavior reveals her true condition. In this particular instance, family support made it possible for the woman to remain in her home. Frequently, however, the patient's disorganization of thought and behavior becomes so severe that home care is no longer feasible.

THE CASE OF MRS. U: A "DOTTY LITTLE OLD LADY"

Mrs. U was a delightful and beautifully dressed 92-year-old widow accompanied by her equally delightful and sparkling 70-year-old daughter. They came from a family of considerable means, and hired caretakers, together with the close supervision of her daughter, a retired professional, enabled Mrs. U to remain at home. Mother and daughter spent time together on a nearly daily basis and often traveled together. The daughter was both attentive and devoted to her aging mother.

Mrs. U was the model of a charming little old lady. She sat primly in her chair, hands folded demurely in her lap, smiling pleasantly and making eye contact. She thanked the physician for seeing her and graciously admired his office decor. Nevertheless, Mrs. U had a profound dementia of the Alzheimer's type. She had absolutely no idea of where she was, the day of the week, or the season. She could not remember anything told to her after a few minutes. She did not know her address, telephone number, or even her birth date. She knew her daughter's name but forgot the names of her other children and knew none of her grandchildren's names. She was unable to draw a clock face or copy a simple triangular figure. For nearly every question put to her, she turned and sweetly asked her daughter to provide the answer.

None of these deficiencies posed a serious problem during daylight hours. But Mrs. U seemed to undergo a severe change in personality in the evening and at night, which was the reason for the consultation. No longer sweet and gracious, she became irritable, intrusive, and violent, screaming and accusing her daughter, caretakers, and any visitors of trying to harm her and steal her money. She paced the floors, had difficulty falling asleep, and was often up in the middle of the night banging on doors and wandering throughout the house. Doors had to be locked to prevent her from leaving the house and wandering down streets, where, unable to find her way back, she would march over to neighbors' houses, bang on their doors and windows, and accuse *them* of trying to hurt her. At times she would talk to her deceased husband while stuffing herself with a wide variety of foods as she stood in front of the open refrigerator.

While these behaviors appear extreme, they are not unusual, and illustrate why older people at this stage of dementia generally have to be placed in nursing homes or residential facilities.

TREATMENT OF DEMENTIA

There is obviously great interest in the development of treatments for memory disturbances. Over the past several decades, numerous medications as well as naturally occurring substances have been used to treat the forgetfulness of normal aging and the severely impaired memory that characterizes dementia. Despite many promising drugs, however, no medication or treatment can cure dementia at this point in time, although some treatments can slow its progression and modestly improve memory. Two medications are currently available for the treatment of dementia in the United States: Cognex (tacrine) and Aricept (donepezil). Their doses and dose ranges are shown in Table 6.2.

Since the effects of these drugs develop slowly over several months, it is important for caregivers and clinicians to help families understand that a long-term commitment to their use is necessary. As they are relatively expensive (approximately $8 per pill), this also means spending a substantial amount of money.

Cognex was the first medication approved by the Food and Drug Administration for treatment of dementia. Its effect in improving the memory impairment of dementia is modest, and for some older individuals, its use is associated with many side effects. The newer drug,

TABLE 6.2. Medications for the Treatment of Dementia

Drug	Dose range
Cognex (tacrine)	40–160 mg/day
Aricept (donepezil)	5–10 mg/day

Aricept, has fewer side effects and appears to be somewhat more effective than Cognex in improving memory and concentration.

Although Aricept may be more effective and safer than Cognex, it, too, has significant side effects (more common with 10 mg/day than with 5 mg). Nausea, vomiting, and diarrhea occur in approximately 10–20% of patients, and muscle cramping and fatigue in approximately 8–10%. Despite these side effects, Aricept is now widely prescribed to patients with Alzheimer's disease and other forms of dementia. Research studies suggest that Aricept does not actually improve memory as much as it delays a downward decline in cognitive functions associated with dementia (Schneider & Tariot, 1998).

In addition to Cognex and Aricept, a variety of other agents that may have modest efficacy are also given to older individuals with dementia. These include estrogen, vitamin E, ginkgo biloba, and nonsteroidal antiinflammatory medications (such as Motrin) (see Table 6.3).

Like the prescription medications, these treatments do not cure Alzheimer's disease but may modestly delay its worsening. None can actually reduce memory impairment, and it is unlikely that any of them is a beneficial treatment for severe dementia. Many older individuals now take vitamin E routinely, although probably at doses that are too low to produce a meaningful response. Because long-term use of nonsteroidal antiinflammatory drugs can cause a variety of gastroin-

TABLE 6.3. Substances That May Have Therapeutic Benefit in Treating Dementia

Substance	Dose
Estrogen	0.65 mg/day
Ginkgo biloba	120 mg twice a day
Vitamin E	2,000 units

Antiinflammatory medications
    Motrin
    Aleve
	Usual daily doses

testinal upsets or even a peptic ulcer, their use in an older individual must be closely supervised by a physician.

TREATMENT OF BEHAVIORAL DISORDERS ASSOCIATED WITH DEMENTIA

Dementia causes a variety of symptoms in addition to memory impairment, the most significant of which are psychosis and disruptive behavior. Psychotic symptoms appear as dementia worsens, generally in the form of paranoid thinking. Examples of paranoid thinking associated with dementia include the following:

- "My spouse is being unfaithful to me."
- "Neighbors/caretakers are trying to harm me."
- "My bank accounts are being looted." (They may sometimes be taken over by concerned children.)
- "My (husband, daughter, son) is an imposter."

Paranoid delusions are typically accompanied by agitation and behavioral disinhibition (worse at night), often with screaming, throwing of objects, or even physical assaults. Under these circumstances, medications to control behavior are necessary. Drugs used to treat agitated patients with dementia are shown in Table 6.4. A more extensive discussion of these medications can be found in Chapter 7.

Atypical neuroleptics are currently the first-choice medications for the treatment of older patients with agitation and dementia because they are particularly helpful with psychotic thinking. When they are ineffective or produce serious side effects, however, other medications shown in Table 6.4 may be used. Depakote (valproate) and Tegretol (carbamazepine) have recently been recommended for severe anger associated with Alzheimer's disease; Desyrel (trazodone) is very useful for agitation.

Physicians and caregivers must also keep in mind that a variety of nonpharmacological techniques can be employed to diminish agitation in the elderly. Some of these are the same as techniques that one would use to reassure a frightened toddler. Remaining calm, consis-

TABLE 6.4. Pharmacological Treatment of Agitation in Patients with Dementia

Class of drugs	Examples of drugs[a]	Dose range
Typical neuroleptics	Haldol (haloperidol)	0.25–2 mg/day
	Trilafon (perphenazine)	2–8 mg/day
	Mellaril (thioridazine)	10–100 mg/day
Atypical neuroleptics	Risperdal (risperidone)	0.25–2 mg/day
	Zyprexa (olanzapine)	2.5–15 mg/day
	Seroquel (quetiapine)	25–100 mg/day
Antidepressants	Desyrel (trazodone)	25–100 mg/day
	SSRI antidepressants	Varies; see Chapter 2 or 7
Anticonvulsants	Depakote (valproate)	125–750 mg/day
	Tegretol (carbamazepine)	200–800 mg/day
	Neurontin (gabapentin)	300–1,800 mg/day
Miscellaneous	Buspar (buspirone)	20–80 mg/day

[a]Only commonly used drugs are shown.

tent, and not leaving the older person alone (which can be terrifying) are helpful. Large orienting cues that are clearly displayed, such as clocks, family photographs with names attached, and signs on doors, are both practical and reassuring. Music, especially from childhood, that is familiar to the older person can be remarkably soothing, and caretakers have long observed that pets tend to quiet the person with agitated dementia. The presence of family members is sometimes calming and sometimes increases agitation. Whenever possible, the person with dementia should not be placed in a situation or asked a question that would emphasize cognitive impairment and thus elicit irritability or agitation.

A more complete description of the use of medication to manage agitation and psychosis can be found in Chapter 7. The following case example traces the progression of Alzheimer's disease, evidenced by deterioration of thinking and memory, and a worsening of behavior. Medication actually helped slow this patient's cognitive deterioration and diminished her agitation.

THE CASE OF MRS. V: MEDICATION MODERATING THE PROGRESSION OF ALZHEIMER'S DISEASE

Mrs. V, age 72, was brought to a psychiatrist by her son and daughter because she was forgetful. She had been a very active though somewhat irritable woman who enjoyed a full social and family life. Her physical health had always been excellent, and she still took pleasure in walking and swimming daily. She was also an accomplished pianist who enjoyed playing the classical repertoire with great ease.

Mrs. V had always kept an accurate accounting of her financial status, travel schedules, and family social arrangements. Following the death of her husband several years earlier, Mrs. V's children began to notice that she seemed increasingly forgetful and less able to organize and plan trips. She noticed the memory loss herself but considered it to be "just old age." As the years passed, however, her memory slipped more noticeably. She was progressively less able to pay her bills on time, and she stopped balancing her checkbook. She often spent hours packing and unpacking for a trip, appearing unable to decide which clothes would be appropriate. Reminiscing more about the past, she seemed less interested in, and somewhat confused by, the ongoing events of her daily life.

Gradually, Mrs. V became so forgetful and disoriented that her children expressed concern for her safety. Because her physical health and energy level were still excellent, the children did not want to put her in an assisted-living facility, and arranged instead for a home healthcare worker to be present during the day. Mrs. V was able to continue her swimming and walking, and with her assistant, she shopped and prepared food for herself. The healthcare worker noticed, however, that Mrs. V was frequently confused about where she was and often dressed inappropriately. She also noticed that Mrs. V made frequent comments about others trying to cheat her.

By the time Mrs. V was 80, she had become quite agitated, especially at night. Awakening in the middle of the night, she would often start yelling at the neighbors through the apartment walls or banging on the ceiling with a broom handle. She got into frequent arguments with neighbors and friends of many years, and her dress became increasingly bizarre. Nevertheless, she continued to swim, walk, and maintain excellent physical health.

By age 82, there was no longer any doubt that Mrs. V had Alzheimer's disease. She repeated herself continually, seemed to forget virtually everything that was said to her within a few minutes, and sometimes did not recognize her children. She needed help preparing food, although she was able to eat without assistance and continued to use the bathroom by herself. Her sleep was regularly disrupted, and she no longer attempted to travel, engage in social activities, or play the piano.

Because of her agitation, Mrs. V was given a low dose of Haldol (haloperidol, 0.5 mg) first only at night and then during the day as well (see Chapter 7). Her restlessness decreased, but she appeared sedated, having lost the sparkle in her facial expression and speech. The dose of Haldol was decreased to 0.25 mg at nighttime, and Aricept (donepezil, 10 mg) was added. After several months of taking Aricept, both Mrs. V's caretaker and her children noticed that she did not seem to be deteriorating any further. In fact, she displayed less paranoid thinking and agitated behavior. Her memory was not substantially improved and she continued to repeat herself, but she appeared better oriented and no longer misidentified her children. Travel arrangements to visit her children and grandchildren often provoked great anxiety but were again possible. There were no side effects, and she was continued on this combination of medications.

The progression of Mrs. V's symptoms is characteristic of Alzheimer's disease. Medications are used to treat two elements of the disease: agitation and memory impairment. Neuroleptics are very effective for controlling agitation, but some older Alzheimer's disease sufferers are unusually sensitive to the side effects and may become overmedicated even at surprisingly low doses.

TREATMENT OF DISRUPTED SLEEP IN PATIENTS WITH DEMENTIA

Since disturbed sleep generally worsens daytime agitation, it is all the more important for individuals with dementia to sleep well. The first principle in treating sleep disorders associated with dementia is to determine whether or not there is a treatable cause of the sleep disturbance. Stimulating medications, excessive caffeine, nicotine, and alcohol contribute to an impaired ability to fall asleep or stay asleep. Other factors (discussed in greater detail in Chapter 5) include pain, breathing difficulties, and the need for frequent urination.

In an effort to help the older patient with dementia sleep well, there is a risk of overmedicating, even when prescribing doses that would be acceptable for a healthy elderly person. Individuals with dementia are often especially sensitive to sedating medications causing paradoxical agitation, disorientation, and confusion. High doses may also produce excessive sedation that causes daytime drowsiness and lethargy that in turn increase social isolation, confusion, disorientation, and agitation.

Medications used to help elderly patients with dementia sleep are the same as those described in Chapter 5, with the exception of benzodiazepines, barbiturates, and nonbarbiturate hypnotics, all of which should not be used because of the possibility of heightened agitation. In rare circumstances, however, a benzodiazepine may be the only medication that helps an older person with dementia sleep. If so, a short half-half compound should be used at the lowest effective dose.

TREATMENT OF DEPRESSION IN PATIENTS WITH DEMENTIA

Treating a depression that accompanies an age-associated memory impairment (or even mild states of dementia) often results in improvement of both cognitive function and depression. Research studies of TCAs and SSRI antidepressants have reported that these medications modestly improve memory in depressed elderly individuals (Gottfries, Karlsson, & Nyth, 1995; Reifler et al., 1989). It is probable that other antidepressants also mildly enhance cognitive function while effectively treating depressive symptoms. However, an older person with depression and dementia will become more agitated if given antidepressant doses that are too high, or drugs that have stimulating properties (such as Norpramin, Prozac, and Wellbutrin). Furthermore, the anticholinergic properties of TCAs may actually worsen memory in some individuals (see Chapter 2). SSRI antidepressants, however, do not have significant anticholinergic properties. Well tolerated in the elderly, they are usually the first-choice medications to treat depression in persons with dementia. As always, the "Start low and go slow" principle should be followed in the dosing regimen.

Late-life depression can affect short-term recall, concentration, and attention. When these cognitive impairments are superimposed upon a developing dementia, the older person may appear even more demented. Once the depression is successfully treated, there is an apparent lessening of the dementia symptoms as the patient's memory improves. Cognitive functions do not return to a predementia level, however, but only to the level that was present before the depression developed. Nevertheless, this improvement is usually experienced as significant—and welcome—by caretakers and family members, as illustrated by the case of Mrs. W.

THE CASE OF MRS. W: LIFTING THE DEPRESSIVE VEIL FROM DEMENTIA

Mrs. W, an 83-year-old widow living alone with the help of her attentive family, began to notice that she was growing both more forgetful and occasionally disoriented. At times, she forgot her shopping lists, did not pay bills, and made incorrect purchases, each of which caused her considerable distress. She noticed her own decline in memory, names in particular, including those of her grandchildren. As her memory worsened, she grew increasingly despondent. When the family members visited her, she would comment that there was nothing left to live for now that she was "losing [her] mind." She did not want to go into a nursing home and spoke of a wish to be dead.

A psychiatrist diagnosed Mrs. W as having depression as well as a dementia, and prescribed low doses of an SSRI antidepressant.

Within 2 weeks, Mrs. W's mood was considerably brighter and there was a noticeable improvement in her memory. Now, rather than withdrawing from her friends, Mrs. W began to seek out their company, and she resumed her shopping and bill paying as well. She acknowledged that she was forgetful but felt able to cope with her memory loss in a more acceptable manner.

TREATMENT OF ANXIETY IN PATIENTS WITH DEMENTIA

Older individuals with dementia are frequently anxious, especially in the early stages of their illness. It is not surprising or unusual to hear them express concern about failing mental abilities and becoming a burden to loved ones or a financial drain on a family. However, the growing anxiety that is often left unspoken beneath these altruistic concerns is more basic and more frightening—the horror of what it will be like to be unable to care for oneself and to lose one's mind.

In the early stages of dementia, reassurance and loving support are helpful and effective. As the disease progresses and anxiety increases, however, medication is necessary. Antianxiety agents are described in Chapter 4, and, as with the treatment of sleep disturbances in patients with dementia, benzodiazepines should be avoided.

The most commonly used nonbenzodiazepine medications to treat anxiety in demented patients are low doses of sedating SSRI anti-depressants when depressive symptoms are also present and atypical neuroleptics. When anxiety, a subjective experience, begins to shift to agitation, an observable behavior, low-dose atypical neuroleptics can be very helpful. Besides controlling disruptive or restless behavior, these medications may also provide the patient with a measure of calm and comfort.

Chapter 7

AGITATION AND PSYCHOSIS

Agitation is one of the more common clinical problems faced by caretakers and clinicians who treat older people. More than mere restlessness, the term **agitation** encompasses severely disruptive, intrusive, or aggressive behavior. Examples of serious agitated behaviors that warrant drug treatment include pacing, wandering, constant irritability, and assaultiveness. Sometimes the agitation manifests only verbally as shouting or screaming; at other times, there are actual physical attacks. The condition usually worsens at night (hence the term **sundowners syndrome**). In most cases, it is the emergence of agitated behavior that necessitates placement in a nursing home or residential facility. The appearance of agitation varies considerably from person to person. For example, some nursing home residents are quiet and well-behaved until a family member visits, and then they begin screaming. Others are noisy and disorderly until a visit by a relative, at which point they become calm, well behaved, and appropriate.

CAUSES OF AGITATION AND PSYCHOSIS

There are multiple causes of agitation and the psychotic thinking that may generate or accompany it. It is important to determine whether the agitated behavior is the result of a brain dysfunction, as in dementia or preexisting psychiatric illness, or of a medical illness such as pulmonary dysfunction. Environmental stress, reaction to one or more medications, or any of these in combination can serve as precipitating factors.

Psychosis commonly occurs in the elderly. It may be brought on by medical illness, dementia, medication side effects, or appear as a component of a psychiatric illness such as depression, mania, schizophrenia, or delusional disorder (paranoia). Agitation as a consequence of psychosis can be distinguished from severe anxious restlessness by the presence of an impaired ability to discern reality and delusions or fragmented thinking. It can be further differentiated from the excitement of mania by the appearance of fear, apprehension, and restlessness without elevated mood, increased rate of speech, or grandiosity. Because agitation and psychosis so commonly accompany one another, their treatment is often the same. For this reason, they are considered together in this chapter.

Agitated behavior accompanied by psychotic delusions usually worsens when a well-meaning person tries to convince the patient that the delusional beliefs are untrue. Late-life delusions often focus on themes of marital infidelity, stolen money, abandonment by family members, or even the belief that a loved one is an imposter. Under the influence of such delusions, older patients with agitation might kick, bite, scream, or hit. Since they rarely respond to reason, medication becomes necessary.

Common psychiatric causes of agitation and psychosis are shown in Table 7.1.

TABLE 7.1. Psychiatric Causes of Agitation and Psychosis

- Dementia
- Delirium
- Delusional disorder
- Schizophrenia
- Major mood disorders

Dementia

Dementia, a leading cause of late-life agitation, usually increases as the illness progresses in severity. Hallucinations, difficulty integrating thoughts and feelings, paranoid thoughts, and misinterpretation of reality are common. As individuals with dementia become more disoriented and confused, paranoid delusions and thinking, fearfulness, and belligerent outbursts increase. Patients cannot be reassured about the safety of their environment or even the reliability and identity of their family members or caretakers. At this stage of dysfunction, agitation is almost inevitable. In nursing homes, the screaming, pleading, or moaning patient with dementia in a gerichair is an all-too-frequent and heartbreaking sight. The progression of illness and accompanying increased agitation is illustrated by the following case vignette.

THE CASE OF MRS. X: AGITATION FOLLOWING PLACEMENT IN NURSING HOME

Mrs. X, 88 years old, had lived a life of considerable artistic and cultural achievement. Her memory began to slip when she was in her 60s and became noticeable in her early 70s. At age 75, she was no longer able to read, write, or participate in any of the cultural activities she had known so well. By age 80, she recognized only her daughter and needed help feeding herself and getting dressed.

After an agonized year of discussion, the family decided to place Mrs. X in a nursing home with special facilities for patients with Alzheimer's disease. Physical and neurological examinations, together with a psychiatric consultation, confirmed the diagnosis of Alzheimer's disease. As Mrs. X was no longer able to make rational decisions on her own behalf, her daughter was appointed legal guardian, and Mrs. X was moved to a nursing home near her daughter's house.

Almost immediately, Mrs. X's behavior began to deteriorate. During the day, she would shout at the nurses or at any person who passed by her room. Tottering out, she would grab on to anyone she could get hold of and scream at them, often incomprehensibly. At night, she sometimes attacked nurses or other nursing home residents. Her sleep was interrupted and fitful. She was unable to eat in the dining room and could not participate in any of the nursing home activities. The only times she was calm was when her daughter visited.

The nursing home staff understood that such a marked increase in agitation was not unusual in patients with Alzheimer's disease who were taken from home and placed in a new environment. They tried gently to reassure Mrs. X and help her learn her way in the new setting. But Mrs. X became even more agitated and more confused, particularly at night. Despite family protests, she was ultimately transferred to a psychiatric hospital for further treatment. This is not an unusual outcome if severe agitation is not adequately treatable in a nursing home setting.

Delirium

Delirium, which also causes agitation, develops more rapidly than dementia. It initially manifests as fluctuations in consciousness accompanied by marked confusion, disorientation, and memory loss. Delirium in the elderly is almost always a result of the onset or worsening of a medical illness, or a reaction to medication. Common causes of delirium in the elderly are as follows:

- Anticholinergic medications
- Dehydration or electrolyte imbalance
- Congestive heart failure
- Infections, especially urinary and respiratory
- Postoperative states

Delirium may also resemble dementia, since it often includes paranoid thinking as well as visual and tactile hallucinations. The confusing and frightening problems commonly experienced by an elderly person with delirium who takes multiple medications are illustrated by the following case.

THE CASE OF MR. Y: MEDICATION-INDUCED DELIRIUM

Mr. Y had been a thoughtful and serious high school teacher for most of his life. Never known to be irrational, suspicious, or inappropriate in his behavior, he spent his retirement years quietly pursuing hobbies, consulting, and teaching inner-city children in a voluntary program. At age 74, Mr. Y was diagnosed with stomach cancer that required immediate surgery. He underwent a 5-hour surgical procedure, which he tolerated well. In the recovery room, however, he seemed unusually confused. Twenty-four hours later, he was disoriented and markedly confused, although in good humor. When asked the name of the President by the attending physician, he pretended to be offended and in a very dignified tone, his eyes wide and his brow furrowed, replied, "Young man, I was a teacher and it is beneath my dignity to answer such a foolish question." He actually had no idea who the President was. His attempt to distract the questioner by providing a misleading answer, known as **confabulation**, is very typical of older patients who are delirious.

Over the next few days, Mr. Y's medical condition improved and he was transferred from the recovery unit to a regular hospital room. But his confusion persisted, and his behavior worsened in the evening. The nurses reported that he had attacked some of the female staff, screamed that he was being poisoned, and tried to pull the intravenous tubes out of his arms. Mr. Y's son, a physician himself, noted that the combination of antidepressant and neuroleptic medication his father was taking might be contributing to his confusion. After a discussion with the surgeon, these medications were discontinued. One week later, Mr. Y's symptoms of delirium had vanished; he was once again calm and lucid, and retained no memory of his fears and agitated behavior.

Delusional Disorder

Delusional disorder (frequently called **paranoia**) is common in late life and, when severe, causes agitation and disruptive behavior. Paranoid thinking may be part of a schizophrenic process (**paranoid schizophrenia**), part of a dementia (see Chapter 6), or may be a psychotic process in its own right, in which case it is known as **delusional disorder**. Regardless of etiology, recurrent themes, discussed in Chapter 6, are characteristic: (1) The patient's money has been stolen; and (2) the patient's spouse is having an affair. Paranoid thinking is also evident when older patients begin to fight with neighbors, bring unnecessary lawsuits, and change their wills. Sometimes the paranoia is an extreme response to understandable concerns of the older person. For example, when family members feel that their elderly relative can no longer manage finances and wish to obtain legal guardianship, the individual's outrage at having lost control of financial affairs and accusations of callous greed may be justified. However, when such thoughts are accompanied by inappropriate aggressive and assaultive behavior, medication is necessary even if realistic family problems exist.

There are elderly patients (particularly, very elderly) who sometimes develop a single delusion. If not asked specifically about the delusion, they appear perfectly normal. Once the delusion is articulated, however, there is little doubt that psychotic thinking is present. Such was the case of Mrs. Z.

THE CASE OF MRS. Z: SINGLE-DELUSION PARANOIA

Mrs. Z was a charming and sophisticated woman of 88. She had never seen a psychiatrist and denied previous psychiatric illness or symptoms. Even following admission to a psychiatric hospital, she continued to maintain that there was nothing wrong with her.

Mrs. Z's symptoms were unique. She pointed to the brown liver spots on the backs of her hands and forehead, and proclaimed these to be butterflies that had somehow been implanted in her skin. She identified the crumbs of breakfast toast that remained around her mouth as the eggs of these butterflies. Such delusional thoughts would not have led Mrs. Z to the hospital except that she was also convinced that family members who wanted her money were implanting the butterflies and their eggs in her skin while she slept. Consequently, she attempted to stay awake at night, becoming agitated, and often yelling. No amount of reassurance or explanation could calm her, and she became even more disquieted when family members tried to reassure her of their innocence.

Mrs. Z was not otherwise delusional, and she was not demented. Like other very elderly patients with similar symptoms, she was treated with a variety of low-dose neuroleptic medications. Although none was particularly useful in decreasing the delusional thinking, they all helped calm her and reduce her nighttime agitation.

Schizophrenia

Schizophrenia in late life is usually the extension of a lifelong illness that began in the patient's early 20s. Symptoms of late-life schizophrenia do not differ from those seen in younger adults, although paranoid thought content is more commonly present. Elderly patients with lifelong schizophrenia are emotionally impaired, unable to live independently, and chronically psychotic. They reside in nursing homes or shuttle between halfway houses, or other supervised residential facilities, and hospitals. Since their cognitive abilities are often seriously impaired, they may appear to be demented as well as psychotic.

A form of paranoid psychosis that appears after age 40 and persists into late life has been variously called **late paraphrenia**, or **late-onset schizophrenia**. That these patients are psychotic is indicated by their predominantly paranoid delusions, but they differ from early-onset schizophrenic patients in having less deteriorated cognition and better social functioning prior to the onset of their psychosis.

Major Mood Disorders

These disorders have been described in detail elsewhere in this book (see Chapters 2 and 3). Manic agitation is usually accompanied by rapid speech, irritability, grandiosity, and a decreased need for sleep. Older patients who are manic have almost always had prior manic episodes, making the diagnosis relatively obvious. When agitated elderly patients with mania become inappropriately aggressive, violent, or paranoid in the presence of caretakers, family members, and clinicians, contact should be limited until medication begins to take effect and calm the agitation.

When agitation is an element of depression, it takes the more classic appearance of pacing, hand wringing, hair pulling, and garment rending. Accompanying these behaviors are sighing, expressions of hopelessness, or even delusions combined with a look of dejection. Depressive agitation may alternate with a state of withdrawal, lack of activity, and near catatonia. Sometimes, the depressed elderly patient barely speaks but is restless nevertheless. Symptoms of depression, as well as a history of prior episodes, present a relatively straightforward diagnostic picture.

TREATMENT OF AGITATION AND PSYCHOSIS

Several classes of medications are used to treat psychotic thinking and agitated behavior in older people. The most common of these are the neuroleptic drugs used to treat psychosis and schizophrenia in younger people. In older people, however, they are also used to treat behavioral outbursts and severe agitation, and psychotic thinking. For this reason, older people are sometimes overmedicated with neuroleptics, especially in nursing homes, and thus experience unnecessary side effects. Unfortunately, because agitation is often a persistent symptom, more or less indefinite treatment with neuroleptics is indicated.

Typical Neuroleptic Medications

Two broad categories of neuroleptics are used to treat agitation and psychosis: typical and atypical. Typical neuroleptics have been used for more than three decades and, until recently, were the first-choice drugs—particularly Haldol (haloperidol) and Mellaril (thioridazine)—for the treatment of serious agitation, inappropriate and disruptive behaviors, and psychotic thinking. Unfortunately, they produce a wide range of side effects, particularly in the elderly. The most commonly used typical neuroleptics are shown in Table 7.2.

Common typical neuroleptic side effects are oversedation and unsteadiness, and anticholinergic side effects, which include dry mouth, constipation, blurred vision, prostate disorders, and in extreme cases, delirium (see Chapter 2). The most distressing typical neuroleptic side effects are known as **extrapyramidal symptoms (EPS)**. These are

TABLE 7.2. Typical Neuroleptics Used for the
Treatment of Agitation and Psychosis in the Elderly

Drug	Dose range
Mellaril (thioridazine)	10–100 mg/day
Trilafon (perphenazine)	2–12 mg/day
Haldol (haloperidol)	0.25–2 mg/day

more common in older people, especially when treated with high doses. EPS are quite easily recognizable: immobile facial appearance, wooden and slow movements, and a muscular restlessness, known as **akathisia**. Tremors, particularly in the hands when at rest, are also common, as is a parkinsonian shuffling gait with small unsteady steps resembling Parkinson's disease. Older people are more sensitive to the development of EPS, especially those who are very old and very frail. In order to minimize side effects, therefore, very low doses of typical neuroleptics are recommended. Even with very low doses, however, EPS may still occur.

Tardive dyskinesia is another EPS that results from typical neuroleptic drugs taken over prolonged periods. This is a syndrome of abnormal movements, usually located around the mouth and face, taking the form of puckering or blowing of the lips and cheeks, rapid flicking of the tongue, grimacing, and frequent involuntary blinking. In severe cases, there are also writhing choreiform movements of the limbs and trunk.

Although EPS are common and distressing, they need not necessarily deter clinicians from prescribing neuroleptics. Disruptive agitated behavior and psychotic thinking can often be controlled by using very small (even minimal) doses. Haldol, the most widely used typical neuroleptic prescribed for control of late-life psychosis and agitation, can serve as an illustration of therapeutic dosage reduction in the elderly. The usual recommended doses for younger and middle-aged adults (4–16 mg/day) will cause virtually all older patients to develop EPS. A fraction of these younger adult daily doses—that is, 0.25–0.5 mg two to four times a day—are effective, with significantly fewer severe side effects. Creative techniques must be employed by caretakers to administer these tiny doses, however. Some typical neuroleptics (Haldol is one) are available in liquid form. Using a tiny syringe (e.g., a TB syringe), the liquid can be introduced into juice or applesauce for the older person.

Concerns about overprescription of typical neuroleptic medications in nursing homes and their resulting side effects motivated the U.S. Congress to pass the Nursing Home Reform Amendment of the Omnibus Reconciliation Act (OBRA) of 1987, which regulates their use. By limiting the prescription of neuroleptics only to those nursing home residents who are psychotic, and by providing dosing guidelines more appropriate for geriatric patients, these regulations have substantially reduced the excessive use of neuroleptics.

Atypical Neuroleptics

Recently, several new neuroleptics with significantly fewer side effects have been developed. These are beginning to replace the typical neuroleptics as first-choice treatments for severe agitation, disruptive behavior, and psychotic thinking in the elderly (see Table 7.3).

The great advantage of these atypical neuroleptics is the relative absence of EPS, which, if they occur at all, tend to be infrequent and extremely mild. Tardive dyskinesia is almost unknown with these medications. However, each can produce its own array of other side effects. Physicians and caretakers need to be familiar with the side-effect profiles of these drugs in order to adjust doses.

Clozaril (clozapine) is very sedating and also produces anticholinergic side effects. Because it also can cause agranulocytosis, which is dangerous and even life-threatening, Clozaril is not usually given to older people. In a recent clinical report, Clozaril may have impaired respiration in a number of older people who were given high doses to control their agitation or psychosis (Salzman et al., 1995). Clozaril also causes substantial weight gain as well as orthostatic hypotension at usual therapeutic doses.

TABLE 7.3. Atypical Neuroleptics for the Treatment of Agitation and Psychosis in the Elderly

Drug	Dose range
Clozaril (clozapine)	12.5–100 mg/day
Risperdal (risperidone)	0.25–1 mg/day
Zyprexa (olanzapine)	2.5–15 mg/day
Seroquel (quetiapine)	25–100 mg/day

Risperdal (risperidone) is now widely used to treat agitated and/ or psychotic elderly patients. One mg/day is the best dose for controlling agitation; in higher doses, Risperdal (like Haldol), begins to produce more severe EPS.

Zyprexa (olanzapine), also now widely used, is effective at relatively low doses (2.5–10 mg/day), although sometimes slightly higher doses may be necessary. It tends to be mildly sedating and may cause mild anticholinergic side effects. Zyprexa is associated with significant weight gain in some individuals.

Seroquel (quetiapine) has a broad effective-dose range (25–100 mg/day). It may cause unsteadiness and orthostatic hypotension.

Antidepressant Medications

A variety of antidepressant medications are useful in diminishing late-life agitation, although they are not used to treat psychosis. The medications and their doses are shown in Table 7.4. Buspar (buspirone), an

TABLE 7.4. Antidepressant Medications Used to Treat Agitation

Drug	Dose range
Atypical antidepressant Desyrel (trazodone)	25–75 mg/day
SSRI antidepressants[a] Paxil (paroxetine) Zoloft (sertraline) Luvox (fluvoxamine) Celexa (citalopram)	5–20 mg/day 12.5–150 mg/day 25–100 mg/day 5–10 mg/day
Buspar (buspirone)[b]	20–80 mg/day

[a]Prozac (fluoxetine) can also be useful in doses of 5–20 mg/ day. However, because it sometimes increases agitation, *very* low starting doses should be used (e.g., 5–10 mg/day).
[b]Buspar is usually considered to be an antianxiety drug rather than an antidepressant. However, it is often effective in controlling agitation caused by dementia.

antianxiety drug, may also diminish agitation, but its results are less reliable than the antidepressants. Each probably achieves its effect by enhancing serotonin function in the brain (see Chapter 2).

Desyrel (trazodone) has the most consistent antiagitation effect of these various medications, although it is very sedating. The sedation tends to wear off over time, but the agitation-reducing properties continue. Desyrel may also cause mild dizziness in some older individuals. Should priapism, a rare but much more serious side effect, develop, the Desyrel must be immediately stopped and not used again.

SSRI antidepressants and Buspar (see Chapters 2 and 4) may also modestly reduce agitation, although they are not as effective as neuroleptics. Recently, SSRIs have been combined with medications such as Aricept (donepezil) to treat the memory impairment of dementia (see Chapter 6). Aricept alone, or combined with an SSRI, may also decrease agitation. However, a few reports of a worsening of behavior with Aricept, especially when used with Risperdal, suggest that this combination should be avoided.

Anticonvulsants

Recently, the antiagitation benefit of anticonvulsants such as Depakote (valproate) and Tegretol (carbamazepine) has been demonstrated in elderly patients. Although these medications do not directly affect psychotic thinking, either may be helpful in controlling agitated behaviors, especially those associated with dementia in late-life manic disorders. As noted in Chapter 6, Depakote (valproate) and Tegretol (carbamazepine) are also effective for the long-term treatment of severe anger associated with dementia. A third anticonvulsant, Neurontin (gabapentin), is also beginning to be used for these disorders. The doses of anticonvulsants used to treat agitation are shown in Table 7.5.

At recommended geriatric doses, Depakote and Tegretol produce very few side effects (see Chapter 3). Depakote has been associated with modest weight gain in younger individuals, and both Depakote and Tegretol may impair concentration and memory when used in very high doses. Because Tegretol accelerates its own metabolism in the liver, doses may need to be readjusted after a few weeks. Neurontin is a very sedating drug; high doses may be associated with falls and daytime sedation.

TABLE 7.5. Anticonvulsants Used to Treat Late-Life Agitation

Drug	Dose range[a]
Depakote (valproate)	125–750 mg/day
Tegretol (carbamazepine)	100–600 mg/day
Neurontin (gabapentin)	300–1,200 mg/day

[a]Effective upper dose limits for these three drugs have not yet been established. The recommendations in this table are to be used as approximate guidelines.

Hormones

Estrogen preparations have been given as experimental treatments to older men (usually with dementia) whose agitation takes the form of inappropriate sexual advances or assaults. Such behavior is highly distressing to other members of a residential facility, as well as to the patient's family, and does not respond well to the traditional treatments for late-life agitation. Estrogen, and even some forms of progesterone, reduce this behavior but cause feminizing side effects. At present, therefore, the use of estrogen to control inappropriate sexual behavior should be considered experimental and initiated only with the consultation and supervision of a psychiatrist.

PRESCRIBING
INFORMATION

The drug doses presented here are meant as recommendations for the approximate ranges for elderly patients. In many cases, the therapeutic range has not been clearly established. Often, older patients respond to doses that are lower than those prescribed for younger patients. Some elderly patients, however, may in fact require usual adult doses or higher doses to experience a therapeutic effect. Side effects such as sedation, postural hypotension, and anticholinergic toxicity are indicators against which dosages must be titrated. Whenever possible, closely following serum levels of medications such as Tegretol, TCAs, lithium, and Depakote is critical because of the greater potential for toxicity at lower doses in older than in younger patients.

TABLE A.1. Psychiatric Drugs

Generic name	Trade name	Approximate daily dose range (mg)	Brief comments
Typical neuroleptics			
Chlorpromazine	Thorazine	10–200	All neuroleptics can cause drows-
Fluphenazine	Prolixin	0.25–4	iness, unsteadiness, restlessness, and stiff muscles. Many of these
Haloperidol	Haldol	0.25–4	drugs will also cause weight
Loxapine	Loxitane	10–100	gain.
Mesoridazine	Serentil	10–200	
Perphenazine	Trilafon	2–32	
Pimozide	Orap	0.25–4	
Thioridazine	Mellaril	10–200	
Thiothixene	Navane	1–15	
Trifluoperazine	Stelazine	1–15	
Atypical neuroleptics			
Olanzapine	Zyprexa	2.5–10	As above.
Quetiapine	Seroquel	25–100	
Risperidone	Risperdal	0.25–2	
Clozapine	Clozaril	10–100	Frequent blood tests are neces- sary when taking clozapine.
Tricyclic antidepressants (TCAs)			
Amitriptyline	Elavil	10–75	All of these drugs can cause
Amoxapine	Asendin	10–300	drowsiness, unsteadiness, dry mouth, constipation, and blurred
Clomipramine	Anafranil	10–250	vision. At high doses, they can
Desipramine	Norpramin	10–75	affect the regularity of heartbeat.
Doxepin	Sinequan, Adapin	10–75	

(continued)

TABLE A.1. *(continued)*

Generic name	Trade name	Approximate daily dose range (mg)	Brief comments
Tricyclic antidepressants *(continued)*			
Imipramine	Tofranil, Aventil	10–75	
Nortriptyline	Pamelor	10–100	
Protriptyline	Vivactil	5–20	
Trimipramine	Surmontil	10–75	
Selective serotonin reuptake inhibitors (SSRIs)			
Citalopram	Celexa	10–40	These antidepressants have fewer side effects than tricyclics. They sometimes cause restlessness, insomnia, and drowsiness.
Fluoxetine	Prozac	5–40	
Fluvoxamine	Luvox	50–150	
Paroxetine	Paxil	5–20	
Sertraline	Zoloft	12.5–150	
Miscellaneous antidepressants			
Bupropion	Wellbutrin	75–225	May cause an increase in energy.
Mirtazapine	Remeron	7.5–45	Very sedating; can cause weight gain.
Nefazodone	Serzone	50–200	Very sedating; potential drug interactions.
Trazodone	Desyrel	25–200	Very sedating and useful as a sleeping pill.
Venlafaxine	Effexor	12.5–225	Can cause nausea and increases in blood pressure.
Monoamine oxidase inhibitors (MAOIs)			
Phenelzine	Nardil	7.5–30	Drug interactions may be serious.
Tranylcypromine	Parnate	5–30	

(continued)

TABLE A.1. *(continued)*

Generic name	Trade name	Approximate daily dose range (mg)	Brief comments
Benzodiazepine anxiolytics			
Alprazolam	Xanax	0.25–2	All can cause drowsiness, unsteadiness, and mild memory impairment. All can cause a mild dependence. Avoid alcohol when using.
Chlordiazepoxide	Librium	10–40	
Clorazepate	Tranxene	3.75–15	
Diazepam	Valium	2–20	
Lorazepam	Ativan	0.25–2	
Oxazepam	Serax	10–45	
Miscellaneous anxiolytics			
Buspirone	Buspar	5–80	
Hydroxyzine	Atarax, Vistaril, Marax	25–100	
Hypnotics			
Estazolam	ProSom	0.5–2	All can cause mild memory loss and confusion upon awakening. Avoid alcohol when using.
Flurazepam	Dalmane	7.5–30	
Quazepam	Doral	7.5–15	
Temazepam	Restoril	7.5–30	
Triazolam	Halcion	0.125–0.25	
Zolpidem	Ambien	5–10	
Mood stabilizers			
Carbamazepine	Tegretol	50–1,200	Can cause decreased white blood cell count; may interact with other medications.
Gabapentin	Neurontin	150–1,200	Sedating; no drug interactions.

(continued)

TABLE A.1. *(continued)*

Generic name	Trade name	Approximate daily dose range (mg)	Brief comments
Mood stabilizers *(continued)*			
Lamotrigine	Lamictal	12.5–50	Can cause serious rash. Dose must be raised slowly.
Lithium	Eskalith, Lithobid	75–1,200	Can cause thirst, increased urination, forgetfulness, and mild tremor.
Valproic acid	Depakene, Depakote	125–1,800	Associated with mild weight gain.
Verapamil	Calan, Isoptin, Verelan	120–480	Can lower blood pressure.
Cognitive enhancers			
Donepezil	Aricept	5–10	Beneficial effect is modest and gradual over several months; mild muscle cramping.
Tacrine	Cognex	20–80	Replaced by Aricept.

Note. From Patel & Salzman (1998). Copyright 1998 by Lippincott Williams & Wilkins. Adapted by permission.

Table A.2. Medical Drugs Interacting with Psychiatric Drugs

Medical drugs	Psychiatric drugs	Side effects
1. Aldomet (methyldopa)	1. Neuroleptics	1. Increase blood pressure, headaches, risk of stroke.
2. Angiotensin–converting enzyme (ACE) inhibitors (Accupril, Aceon, Altace, Capoten, Lotensin, Mavik, Monopril, Prinivil, Univasc, Vasotec, Zestril)	2a. Lithium	2a. Increase lithium levels causing tremor, nausea, confusion, dry hair, increased urination, and increased thirst.
	2b. Neuroleptics	2b. Further lowering of blood pressure.
3. Antiarrhythmics (Cardioquin, Ethmozine, Mexitil, Norpace, Procanbid, Quinaglute, Quinidex, Quinidine, Rythmol, Tambocor, Tonocard)	3a. TCAs	3a. May cause serious heart arrhythmias.
	3b. SSRI antidepressants	3b. Increase blood levels of antiarrhythmics and increase risk of heart arrhythmias.
4a. Antibiotics (doxycycline)	4a. Decrease the antibiotic effect.	4a. Carbamazepine
4b. Antibiotics (erythromycin, troleandomycin)	4b. Carbamazepine	4b. Increase carbamazepine effect with potentially serious heart block.
4c. Erythromycin	4c. Nefazodone	4c. Increase blood levels of nefazodone.
4d. Antibiotics (spectinomycin, tetracycline)	4d. Lithium	4d. Increase lithium effect and lithium side effects.
5. Bromocriptine	5. Neuroleptics	5. Each drug interferes with the therapeutic effect of the other.

(continued)

Table A.2. *(continued)*

Medical drugs	Psychiatric drugs	Side effects
6. Caffeine	6. Fluvoxamine	6. Increase the likelihood of caffeine jitters and sleeplessness.
7. Calcium channel blockers (Adalat, Calan, Cardizem, Isoptin, Nimotop, Norvasc, Plendil, Posicor, Procardia, Sular, Tiazac, Vascor, Verelan)	7. TCAs (Elavil, Tofranil, Sinequan, Norpramin, Adapin, Pertofrane, Anafranil, Aventil)	7. Increase sedation, dizziness, sweating, dry mouth, constipation, blurred vision, urinary retention (increase tricyclic blood levels).
8. Catapres (clonidine)	8a. TCAs (Elavil, Tofranil, Sinequan, Norpramin, Adapin, Pertofrane, Anafranil, Aventil)	8a. Increase blood pressure (block antihypertensive effects).
	8b. Neuroleptics	8b. Cause further decrease in blood pressure; dizziness, unsteadiness.
9. Cough medicine with dextromethorphan (Bromfed DM, Diabe-tuss DM, Dimetane-DX, Duratuss DM, Phenergan with Tussar DM, Safe Tussin, Syn-RX DM, Tussi-Organidin DM, Tylenol cold medication, Tylenol cough medication, Anatuss DM, Benylin, Codimal DM, Donatussin, Fenesin DM, Guafenesin and	9. SSRI antidepressants (Prozac, Zoloft, Paxil, Luvox, Celexa)	9. Flushing, sweating, elevated blood pressure, increased temperature, shakes (serotonin syndrome).

Dextromethorphan, Muco-fen DM, Poly-histine DM, Protuss-DM, Respa-DM, Rondec-DM, Sudafed, Tuss-DM, Tussar DM)		
10a. Coumadin (warfarin)	10a. SSRI antidepressants	10a. Increase risk of bleeding (increased warfarin levels).
10b. Coumadin (warfarin)	10b. Clozapine	10b. Increase tendency toward bleeding.
11. Demerol (meperidine)	11. MAOIs (Nardil, Parnate, Marplan)	11. Increase temperature, sweating, risk of death.
12. Diabetes medication (hypoglycemics)	12a. MAOIs	12a. Further lowering of blood sugar levels.
	12b. Neuroleptics	12b. Can increase blood glucose levels.
13. Diamox (acetazolamide), diuretics (Bumex, Demadex, Edecrin, Lasix, Diucardin, Diuril, Enduron, Hydrodiuril, Microzide, Mykrox, Oratic, Thalitone, Zaroxolyn)	13. Lithium	13. Increase lithium levels, causing tremor, nausea, confusion, dry hair, increased urination, and thirst.
14. Digoxin	14. Clozapine (Clozaril)	14. Increase digoxin levels, causing serious cardiac effects.
15a. Estrogen	15a. Imipramine	15a. Increase imipramine effects, producing lethargy, headache, tremor, and greater decrease in blood pressure.
15b. Estrogen	15b. TCAs (Elavil, Tofranil, Sinequan, Norpramin, Adapin, Pertofrane, Anafranil, Aventil)	15b. Increase sedation, dizziness, sweating, dry mouth, constipation, blurred vision, urinary retention (increase tricyclic blood levels).

(continued)

Table A.2. (*continued*)

Medical drugs	Psychiatric drugs	Side effects
16a. Hismanal, Seldane	16a. Serzone (nefazodone)	16a. Cardiac arrhythmias.
16b. Hismanal (terfenadine), Seldane (astemizole)	16b. SSRI antidepressants	16b. Potentially fatal heartbeat irregularity.
17. Inderal (propranolol)	17. Neuroleptics	17. Increase blood levels of Inderal and further lower blood pressure, causing dizziness and unsteadiness.
18. Ketaconazol–itraconazole	18. Benzodiazepine antianxiety drugs	18. Increase benzodiazepine blood levels, causing significant drowsiness and unsteadiness.
19. Labetalol	19. Imipramine	19. Increase imipramine levels, causing more antidepressant side effects.
20. Nonsteroidal antiinflammatory agents [NSAIDs] (Anaprox, Cataflam, Clinoril, Daypro, Dolobid, Duract, Naprosyn, Ecotrin, Feldene, Indocin, Lodine, Motrin, Nalfon, Naprelan, Orudis, Ponstel, Relafen, Tolectin, Toradol, Voltaren)	20. Lithium	20. Increase lithium blood levels and lithium side effects.
21. Prednisone, Decadron, estrogen	21. Nefazodone	21. Increase steroid blood levels.
22. Propulsid (cisapride)	22. SSRI antidepressants	22. Potentially fatal heartbeat irregularity.

23. Quinidine	23. TCAs (Elavil, Tofranil, Sinequan, Norpramin, Adapin, Pertofrane, Anafranil, Aventil)	Dangerous cardiac arrhythmias; increase sedation, unsteadiness due to higher tricyclic levels.
24. Rifampin	24. Neuroleptics	Can decrease neuroleptic effect.
25. Stimulants (amphetamine, dopamine, Ephedrine, Levateranol, Mephenteramine, Metaraminol, methylphenidate, phenylephrine, phenylpropanolamine, Pseudoephedrine, L-tryptophan, Meperidine [Demerol], L-Dopa)	25. MAOIs (Nardil, Marplan, Parnate)	Increase blood pressure, severe headache, risk of stroke, heart attack. This is a medical emergency. If there is an increase in blood pressure, then taking Regitine (phentolamine) or Procardia (nifedipine) under a doctor's supervision will lower blood pressure and reduce the risks of serious side effects.
26. Tagamet (cimetidine)	26a. TCAs (Elavil, Tofranil, Sinequan, Norpramin, Adapin, Pertofrane, Anafranil, Aventil)	Increase sedation, dizziness, sweating, dry mouth, constipation, blurred vision, urinary retention (increase tricyclic blood levels).
	26b. Benzodiazepines	Increase unsteadiness due to higher benzodiazepine levels; increase sedation, dizziness, sweating, dry mouth, constipation, blurred vision, urinary retention (increase tricyclic blood levels).
27. Tegretol (carbamazepine)	27. TCAs, Serzone, Xanax, Halcion	Decrease blood levels and decrease therapeutic effect.

(continued)

Table A.2. (*continued*)

Medical drugs	Psychiatric drugs	Side effects
28. Theophylline	28. Luvox	28. Rapid heart rate, increased blood pressure, shakiness, jitteriness, sweating.
29. Tylenol	29. Luvox	29. Increase Luvox side effects.
30. Vasopressors (Ana-kit, anaphylaxis emergency treatment kit, Aramine, Epi E–Z pen junior, Neo-Synephrine, ProAmatine, Vasoxyl)	30. MAOIs	30. Increase in blood pressure, increase risk of stroke or heart attack.

Note. From Patel & Salzman (1998). Copyright 1998 by Lippincott Williams & Wilkins. Adapted by permission.

TABLE A.3. Drug Interactions with Psychotropic Medications

Drug	Interacting with	Clinical effect of interaction
Neuroleptics	Guanethidine	Chlorpromazine, haloperidol, thiothixene reverse antihypertensive effects.
	Bethanidine	Decreases antihypertensive effects.
	Debrisoquine	Decreases antihypertensive effects.
	Clonidine	Delirium with fluphenazine. Decreases antihypertensive effects.
	Bromocriptine	Concurrent use may reduce pharmacological effects of each other.
	Caffeine	Can counteract sedation and exacerbate psychosis. May delay clinical effects.
	Oral contraceptive	May increase effect of antipsychotic drugs.
	Anticholinergics	Increase anticholinergic effects. Delay onset of effects of acute oral doses of antipsychotics.
	Beta blockers	May increase levels of either chlorpromazine or beta blockers. Additive hypotensive effects and cardiopulmonary arrest. Can increase plasma concentrations of phenothiazines.
	Epinephrine	Can cause hypotension and tachycardia when used with low-potency antipsychotics (e.g., chlorpromazine and thioridazine).

(continued)

TABLE A.3. (*continued*)

Drug	Interacting with	Clinical effect of interaction
Neuroleptics (*continued*)	Benzodiazepines	Two cases of cardiopulmonary collapse with clozapine. Increase sedation. Increase risk of respiratory depression.
	Carbamazepine	Can decrease neuroleptic levels. Neurotoxicity with haloperidol. Increases risk of granulocytopenia and possibly agranulocytosis with clozapine. Can decrease levels of clozapine.
	SSRIs	Fluoxetine increases levels of some antipsychotics (e.g., clozapine, haloperidol). Fluoxetine increases EPS. Paroxetine can increase clozapine levels. Fluvoxamine significantly increases clozapine levels.
	Cimetidine	Decreases chlorpromazine absorption. Increases sedation with chlorpromazine. Inhibits metabolism of antipsychotics. May increase clozapine levels.
	Lithium	May cause neurotoxicity and delirium-like symptoms. May increase EPS. May decrease chlorpromazine levels, possibly due to inhibition of gastric emptying. May increase lithium excretion with chlorpromazine.

	Ventricular fibrillation associated with chlorpromazine and sudden withdrawal of lithium.
Meperidine	Third-degree heart block with mesoridazine. Central nervous system (CNS) toxicity correlates with antipsychotic dosage.
	CNS toxicity with phenothiazines.
Phenytoin	Phenytoin toxicity may increase. Decreases antipsychotic serum levels.
Chloroquine	Phenothiazines increase chloroquine levels.
Digoxin	Clozapine increases levels of digoxin through protein-binding displacement.
Captopril	Hypotension and postural syncope with chlorpromazine.
TCAs	Increase hypotension, sedation, anticholinergic side effects. Possible ventricular arrhythmias with thioridazine. Possible increase in plasma levels of both drugs. Possible increased risk of seizures. Increased EPS with amoxapine.
L-Dopa	Decreased antiparkinsonian effects of L-Dopa. May exacerbate psychosis.
Amphetamines	Decreased appetite suppression by amphetamines. Decreased effectiveness of amphetamines.

(continued)

TABLE A.3. *(continued)*

Drug	Interacting with	Clinical effect of interaction
Neuroleptics *(continued)*	Oral hypoglycemics	Antipsychotics increase serum glucose; may require dosage adjustment of diabetic medication.
	Phenylpropanolamine	Ventricular arrhythmias with thioridazine. May increase sedation.
	Rifampin	May decrease effect of antipsychotics by increasing their metabolism.
	MAOIs	May increase effect of antipsychotics by decreasing their metabolism. Increased EPS with phenothiazines. Hepatotoxicity and encephalopathy with iproniazid and prochlorperazine. Increased risk of hypotension. Catatonia with haloperidol and phenelzine.
	Warfarin	Clozapine increases levels of warfarin through protein-binding displacement.
	Phenindione	Haloperidol may decrease bleeding via enzyme induction.
	Methyldopa	Orthostatic hypotension. Reversible dementia with haloperidol. Rare delirium. Paradoxical hypertension.
	Enflurane/isoflurane	Profound hypotension with phenothiazines.
	Nefazodone	May increase haloperidol levels.

	Bupropion	May further decrease seizure threshold.
	Narcotics	Increase sedation. Increase hypotension. May increase respiratory depression.
	Indomethacin	May cause drowsiness with haloperidol.
	Valproic acid	Prolongs half-life of chlorpromazine.
	Trazodone	Additive hypotension with phenothiazines.
	Buspirone	May increase haloperidol levels.
TCAs	i.v. epinephrine/i.v. norepinephrine/ i.v. phenylephrine	Significant increase in pressor response to these sympathomimetic drugs.
	Local anesthetic	Increased nasal bleeding during nasal surgery when dissolved in epinephrine.
	Anticholinergics	Additive anticholinergic effects. Risk of anticholinergic delirium.
	Barbiturates	May decrease blood levels of TCAs by inducing hepatic metabolism. Respiratory depressive effects can be additive.
	Beta-adrenergic blockers	Labetalol may increase imipramine levels.
	Carbamazepine	Decreases TCA levels and increases heterocyclic metabolites and toxicity.

(continued)

TABLE A.3. *(continued)*

Drug	Interacting with	Clinical effect of interaction
TCAs *(continued)*	Cimetidine	Increases TCA levels. Risk of psychosis with cimetidine and imipramine.
	Guanethidine	Elevated blood pressure.
	MAOIs	Toxic reaction can occur if TCAs abruptly substituted for MAOIs. Death possible. Disseminated intravascular coagulation with clomipramine. Metabolism inhibited. TCA blood levels and toxicity increased. Increase incidence of mania.
	Oral anticoagulants	Increased bioavailability of dicumarol. Increased bleeding.
	Quinidine	Increases TCA levels. Additive type 1a antiarrhythmic effects.
	SSRIs	Increase TCA levels significantly.
	Valproate	Increased valproate levels.
	Antipsychotics	Possible ventricular arrhythmias with thioridazine. Increase EPS with amoxapine. Possible increase in plasma levels of both drugs. Increase sedation, hypotension, anticholinergic effect. Possible increased risk of seizures.
	Methylphenidate	Increases TCA levels.

Verapamil	Increases TCA levels.
Methadone/morphine	Increased levels of analgesia from both drugs. Increased morphine levels. Increases TCA levels.
Bethanidine	Decreases antihypertensive effects.
Clonidine	Decreases antihypertensive effects. Potential hypertensive crises with imipramine.
Debrisoquine	Decreases antihypertensive effects.
Methyldopa	Agitation, tremor, and tachycardia with amitriptyline.
Lithium	May increase lithium tremor. Seizures with amitriptyline. Myoclonus.
Phenytoin	Induces hepatic metabolism and decreases TCA blood levels.
Estrogen	Decreases therapeutic effect of imipramine. Prolongs half-life of imipramine. Lethargy, headache, tremor, hypotension. Increases incidence of akathisia.
Testosterone	Paranoid psychosis with aggression.
L–Dopa	Increases agitation, tremor, rigidity. Decreases plasma levels via impaired gastrointestinal absorption.

(continued)

TABLE A.3. *(continued)*

Drug	Interacting with	Clinical effect of interaction
TCAs *(continued)*	Benzodiazepines	Increase sedation, confusion, impaired motor function.
	Alcohol	Increases sedation.
		Changes levels of TCA by effects on TCA metabolism.
	Sulfonylureas	Increase incidence of hypoglycemia.
	Procainamide	Prolongs cardiac conduction.
MAOIs	Amphetamines	All increase blood pressure.
	Buspirone	
	Dopamine	
	Ephedrine	
	Levarterenol	
	Mephentermine	
	Metaraminol	
	Methylphenidate	
	Phenylephrine	
	Phenylpropanolamine	

Procaine hydrochloride (dissolved in epinephrine)	Hypertensive crises, strokes, and death.
Pseudoephedrine	
Amine-containing foods	Serotonin syndrome.
L-Tryptophan	Known fatalities; toxic reaction and coma; report of agitation and delirium with selegiline.
Meperidine	
Morphine	Hypotension.
SSRIs	Sudden death secondary to hyperserotonergic states.
Serotonin agonists	5-week interval required between discontinuation of fluoxetine and starting MAOI.
Sympathomimetics	Fatalities, cardiac arrhythmias, hyperpyrexia, and cerebral vascular hemorrhage.
Dextromethorphan	Fatalities and toxic reactions.
Insulin/sulfonylureas	May enhance or prolong hypoglycemic reaction. Both increase hypotension.

(continued)

TABLE A.3. *(continued)*

Drug	Interacting with	Clinical effect of interaction
MAOIs *(continued)*	L-Dopa	Acute hypertension.
	TCAs	Toxic reaction if TCAs added to or abruptly substituted for MAOIs. Fatalities possible. Metabolism inhibited. TCA blood levels and toxicity increased. Disseminated intravascular coagulation with clomipramine. Increase incidence of mania.
	Tranylcypromine	Hypertensive reaction with other MAOIs, particularly if switched abruptly.
	Fenfluramine	Confusion
	Reserpine	Hypomania
	Guanethidine	Decreased antihypertensive effect.
	Alcohol	May induce hypertensive crises. Increases CNS depression. Malignant hyperthermia.
	Amantadine	Elevated blood pressure.
	Lithium	Tardive dyskinesia with tranylcypromine.
	Neuroleptics	Increase risk of hypotension. Increase EPS with phenothiazines.

		May increase effect of antipsychotics by decreasing metabolism. Hepatotoxicity and encephalopathy with iproniazid and prochlorperazine.
	Thiazide diuretics	Increase hypotension.
	Venlafaxine	Toxicity
	Nefazodone	Toxicity
SSRIs	Beta blockers	Metoprolol and fluoxetine increase frequencies of bradycardia. Fluvoxamine increases levels of propranolol.
	Cimetidine	May increase paroxetine levels.
	Cyproheptadine	Loss of antidepressant activity.
	Diuretics	Syndrome of inappropriate secretion of antidiuretic hormone (SIADH) with sertraline and fluoxetine.
	Lithium	Lithium-induced neurotoxicity probably secondary to SIADH from SSRIs. Fever, increased bilirubin, leukocytosis. Fluoxetine increases lithium levels.
	Oral anticoagulants	Increases risk of bleeding. Increases warfarin concentration with fluvoxamine.
	Theophylline	Increased theophylline levels with fluvoxamine may result in coma, seizures, and supraventricular tachycardia.

(continued)

TABLE A.3. *(continued)*

Drug	Interacting with	Clinical effect of interaction
SSRIs *(continued)*	L–Tryptophan	Mild serotonin syndrome. Worsened symptoms of obsessive–compulsive disorder.
	TCAs	Significantly increased TCA levels.
	MAOIs	Serotonin syndrome and fatality. 5-week interval required between discontinuing fluoxetine and starting MAOI.
	Phenytoin	Increased phenytoin levels.
	Hypoglycemic drugs	Increased hypoglycemia, mostly with fluoxetine.
	Type 1c antiarrhythmics	Increased levels of the antiarrhythmics.
	Codeine	Increased codeine levels.
	Terfenadine/ astemizole/ cisapride	Theoretical risk of ventricular arrhythmia.
	Neuroleptics	Fluoxetine increases levels of some antipsychotics (e.g., clozapine, haloperidol). Fluvoxamine significantly increases clozapine levels. Paroxetine may increase clozapine levels. Fluoxetine increases EPS.
	Carbamazepine	Fluoxetine increases levels of carbamazepine.

Miscellaneous antidepressants:		
Nefazodone	Nonsedating antihistamines	Astemizole and terfenadine levels may increase, causing fatal *torsades de pointes*.
	Benzodiazepines	Levels of triazolobenzodiazepines may increase.
	Digoxin	Elevation of digoxin levels.
	Haloperidol	Haloperidol levels may increase.
Venlafaxine	MAOIs	Toxicity
	Cimetidine	Increases levels in at-risk populations.
Bupropion	Neuroleptics	May further decrease seizure threshold.
	TCAs	May further decrease seizure threshold.
Trazodone	Coumadin	Decreases prothrombin times.
	Neuroleptics	Additive hypotension with phenothiazines.
	Thiazide diuretics	Increase lithium levels; may require 50% dose reduction.
	ACE inhibitors	May decrease lithium clearance and increase lithium levels, causing neurotoxicity.
	Carbamazepine	Carbamazepine-induced water intoxication and hyponatremia may cause lithium toxicity. Increased risk of neurotoxicity.

(continued)

TABLE A.3. *(continued)*

Drug	Interacting with	Clinical effect of interaction
Mood stabilizers: Lithium	Iodide salts	May have synergistic action in precipitating hypothyroidism.
	Methyldopa	May cause neurotoxicity due to increased lithium levels.
	Osmotic diuretics	May decrease lithium levels.
	Prostaglandin inhibitors	All can decrease lithium clearance significantly and increase lithium levels.
	Diclofenac	
	Ibuprofen	
	Indomethacin	
	Naproxen	
	Piroxicam	
	Sulindac	
	Ketoralac	
	Phenylbutazone	
	Aspirin	

Theophylline	Decreases lithium levels due to increased renal clearance.
Caffeine	Decreases lithium levels via increased renal clearance.
Aminophylline	Decreases lithium levels via increased renal clearance.
Verapamil	May decrease lithium levels. Sinus bradycardia Choreoathetosis Neurotoxicity
Diltiazem	Increases lithium levels.
Furosemide	Increases lithium effect and toxicity due to decreased renal lithium clearance.
Clonidine	Decreases antihypertensive effect.
Neuroleptics	May cause neurotoxicity and delirium-like symptoms. CNS toxicity correlates with antipsychotic dosage.
Sodium bicarbonate, sodium chloride, urea	All decrease lithium levels via increased renal clearance.
Metronidazole, spectinomycin, tetracycline	All increase lithium effect and toxicity via renal clearance.
Sulfamethoxazole-trimethoprim	Decreases lithium levels.

(continued)

TABLE A.3. *(continued)*

Drug	Interacting with	Clinical effect of interaction
Lithium *(continued)*	TCAs	May increase lithium tremor. Seizures with amitriptyline. Myoclonus
	Digitalis	May cause cardiac arrhythmias by depleting intracellular potassium. Decreases response to lithium.
	SSRIs	Fluoxetine increases lithium levels. Fever, increased bilirubin, leukocytosis with fluoxetine. Lithium-induced neurotoxicity probably due to SIADH from SSRI.
	Insulin	Insulin dosage may need adjustment early in lithium treatment due to altered glucose tolerance.
Other mood stabilizers: Valproic acid	Barbiturates	Possibility of barbiturate intoxication by inhibition of its metabolism.
	Carbamazepine	Both drugs affect each other's levels and require close monitoring.
	Phenytoin	Both drugs affect each other's levels unpredictably.
	Salicylates	May produce more hepatotoxic metabolites of valproate. May cause valproic acid toxicity by increasing free levels and decreasing free clearance.

	Magnesium/ aluminum hydroxide	Increases valproate levels.
	Lamotrigine	Increased lamotrigine levels. Risk of Stevens–Johnson syndrome.
	Benzodiazepines	May increase sedation and "absence" seizure activity. Increases half-life of diazepam.
	Ethosuximide	Prolongs half-life.
	TCAs	Increase valproate levels.
Carbamazepine	Macrolide antibiotics	Erythromycin and troleandomycin may cause significant increase in carbamazepine levels and toxicity, including heart block.
	Neuroleptics	Neuroleptics levels may decrease. Clozapine levels may decrease. Increase risk of granulocytopenia and possibly of agranulocytosis with clozapine. Neurotoxicity with haloperidol.
	Bupropion	Bupropion concentration may decrease.
	Cimetidine	May inhibit carbamazepine metabolism transiently during first week.
	Calcium channel blockers	Neurotoxicity when combined with diltiazem and verapamil but not with nifedipine. May decrease bioavailability of felodipine.

(continued)

TABLE A.3. *(continued)*

Drug	Interacting with	Clinical effect of interaction
Carbamazepine *(continued)*	Corticosteroids	Increase clearance of corticosteroids.
	Cyclosporine	Increases clearance of cyclosporine.
	Danazol	May increase carbamazepine levels significantly and cause neurotoxicity.
	SSRIs	Fluoxetine increases levels of carbamazepine.
	Doxycycline	May increase doxycycline metabolism.
	Isoniazid	May cause toxicity secondary to increased carbamazepine levels.
	Lithium	Increases polyuria, ataxia, and dizziness due to antidiuretic effect of carbamazepine. Increased risk of neurotoxicity.
	Mebendazole	Mebendazole levels may decrease.
	Methadone	Methadone levels may decrease.
	Neuromuscular blocking agents	May shorten postoperative recovery times significantly.
	Oral anticoagulants	Warfarin concentrations may decrease.
	Oral contraceptives	Contraceptive drug levels may decrease and risk of pregnancy increase.
	Propoxyphene	Increases carbamazepine levels and risk of toxicity.

	Theophylline	Both drugs may decrease each other's levels.
	Benzodiazepines	Decreased clonazepam and alprazolam levels.
	Thyroid hormones	May induce metabolism of thyroid replacement hormones.
	TCAs	Decreased TCA levels and increased tricyclic metabolites.
	Valproic acid	Both drugs affect each other's levels and require close monitoring.
	Phenobarbital/phenytoin/primidone	All decrease carbamazepine serum levels.
Benzodiazepines	Itraconazole–ketoconazol	Increase alprazolam, midazolam, and triazolam blood levels significantly.
	Oral contraceptives	Inhibit oxidative metabolism of long-acting benzodiazepines and increase toxicity.
	Calcium channel blockers	Increase half-life of benzodiazepines metabolized by cytochrome P450 3A3/4 enzymes.
	Disulfiram	Inhibits metabolism of some benzodiazepines.
	Erythromycin/troleandomycin	Inhibits midazolam and triazolam metabolism.

(continued)

TABLE A.3. *(continued)*

Drug	Interacting with	Clinical effect of interaction
Benzodiazepines *(continued)*	Alcohol	Increases sedation. Additive CNS depressant effects; ethanol may increase benzodiazepine absorption and impair its elimination. Behavioral dyscontrol and adverse psychomotor effects with alcohol and benzodiazepines.
	Antacids, anticholinergics	All delay oral absorption of benzodiazepines.
	H_2 blockers	Ranitidine may decrease oral diazepam levels. Cimetidine may significantly increase benzodiazepine levels and cause CNS intoxication.
	Probenecid	May increase lorazepam levels significantly.
	Protease inhibitors	Benzodiazepines metabolized by CYP 3A3/4 may have higher levels.
	Rifampin	Increases clearance of benzodiazepines.
	Isoniazid	Increase toxicity of some benzodiazepines due to inhibition of oxidative metabolism.
	Fluoxetine	Increases half-life of diazepam.
	Phenytoin	Decreases clinical effect of benzodiazepines due to hepatic enzymes induction.
	Neuroleptics	Increase risk of respiratory depression. Increase sedation. Two cases of cardiopulmonary collapse with clozapine.

	Barbiturates/narcotics	Increase sedation.
	Valproic acid	May increase sedation and "absence" seizure activity with clonazepam. Increases half-life of diazepam.
	TCAs	Increase sedation, confusion, impaired motor function. Alprazolam may increase TCA levels.
	Nefazodone	May increase levels of triazolobenzodiazepines.
	MAOIs	Disinhibition and generalized edema with chlordiazepoxide.
	Metoprolol	Decreases negative chronotropic effect with chlordiazepoxide.
	Digoxin	Increases digoxin levels with diazepam.
	Carbamazepine	Decreases clonazepam and alprazolam levels.
Buspirone	Haloperidol	Haloperidol levels may increase.
	MAOIs	Increase blood pressure.
	TCAs	Hypertension and anxiety with clomipramine.
Chloral hydrate	Ethanol	Increases CNS depression. May cause unexpected reactions such as flushing, tachycardia, and headache.
	Oral anticoagulants	Effect of warfarin may be potentiated.
	Anticonvulsants	Increase levels of phenytoin and phenobarbital.

(continued)

TABLE A.3. *(continued)*

Drug	Interacting with	Clinical effect of interaction
Methylphenidate	MAOIs	Hypertension
	TCAs	Increased TCA levels.
	Guanethidine	Decreases pressor effect.
	Pressor agents	Increase pressor effect.
Anticholinergic/ antiparkin- sonian agents	Amantadine	May potentiate anticholinergic effects resulting in nocturnal confusion and hallucinations.
	TCAs	Additive anticholinergic effects. Anticholinergic delirium.
	Antipsychotics	May alter antipsychotic blood levels. Delay onset of effects of acute oral doses of antipsychotics. Increase anticholinergic effects. Possible increased risk of hyperthermia. MAOIs may enhance CNS depression.
Cognitive enhancers: Donepezil	Succinylcholine anesthesia	Increased muscle relaxation.

	Atropine and other vagotonic drugs	Bradycardia (do not give to patients with "sick sinus syndrome").
	Nonsteroidal anti-inflammatory drugs	Increase occult gastrointestinal bleeding, especially in those at risk for ulcers.
	Ketaconazol–itraconazole, nefazodone, quinidine, fluoxetine, paroxetine	Possible increase in donepezil blood levels and side effects.
	Carbamazepine, dexamethasone, rifampin, phenobarbital	Possible decrease in donepezil blood levels.
Tacrine	Theophylline	Significantly increased plasma levels of theophylline.
	Cimetidine	Increases tacrine levels.
	Succinylcholine anesthesia	Enhanced anesthetic effects.
	Fluvoxamine	Markedly increases levels of tacrine.

Note. From Patel & Salzman (1998). Copyright 1998 by Lippincott Williams & Wilkins. Adapted by permission.

REFERENCES

Alexopoulos, G. S., Meyers, B. S., Young, R. C., Kakuma, T., Feder, M., Einhorn, A., & Rosendahl, E. (1996). Recovery in geriatric depression. *Archives of General Psychiatry, 53,* 305–312.

American Psychiatric Association. (1994). *Diagnostic and statistical manual of mental disorders* (4th ed.). Washington, DC: Author.

American Psychiatric Association Task Force report on benzodiazepine dependency, toxicity, and abuse. (1990). Washington, DC: American Psychiatric Press.

Avorn, J. (1998). Drug prescribing, drug taking, adverse reactions, and compliance in elderly patients. In C. Salzman (Ed.), *Clinical geriatric psychopharmacology* (3rd ed., pp. 21–47). Baltimore: Williams & Wilkins.

Baldessarini, R. J., Tondo, L., Faedda, G. L., Suppes, T. R., Floris, G., & Rudas, N. (1996). Effects of the rate of discontinuing lithium maintenance treatment in bipolar disorders. *Journal of Clinical Psychiatry, 57,* 441–448.

Baldessarini, R. J., Tondo, L., Suppes, T., Faedda, G. L., & Tohen, M. (1996). Pharmacological treatment of bipolar disorder throughout the life-cycle. In K. I. Shulman, M. Tohen, & S. Kutcher (Eds.), *Bipolar disorder through the life-cycle* (pp. 299–338). New York: Wiley.

Balter, M. B., & Uhlenhuth, E. H. (1992, December). New epidemiologic findings about insomnia and its treatment. *Journal of Clinical Psychiatry, 53,* 34–39, 40–42.

Barbone, F., McMahon, A. D., Davey, P. G., Morris, A. D., Reid, I. C., McDevitt, D. G., & MacDonald, T. M. (1998). Association of road-traffic accidents with benzodiazepine use. *Lancet, 352,* 1331–1336.

Cardakson, M. A., Brown, E. D., & Dement, W. C. (1982). Sleep fragmentation in the elderly: Relationship to daytime sleep tendency. *Neurobiology and Aging, 3,* 321–327.

Edinger, J. D., Hoelscher, T. J., & Marsh, G. R. (1992). A cognitive-behavioral therapy for sleep-maintenance insomnia in older adults. *Psychology and Aging, 7,* 282–289.

Gillin, J. C., & Ancoli-Israel, S. (1998). The impact of age on sleep and sleep disorders. In C. Salzman (Ed.), *Clinical geriatric psychopharmacology* (3rd ed., pp. 371–394). Baltimore: Williams & Wilkins.

Gottfries, C.-G., Karlsson, I., & Nyth, A. L. (1992). Treatment of depression in elderly patients with and without dementia disorders. *International Clinical Psychopharmacology, 6* (Suppl. 5), 55–64.

Hart, R. P., Colenda, C. C., & Hamer, R. M. (1991). Effects of buspirone and alprazolam on the cognitive performance of normal elderly subjects. *American Journal of Psychiatry, 148*, 73–77.

Katz, I. R., Miller, D., & Oslin, D. (1998). Diagnosis of late-life depression. In C. Salzman (Ed.), *Clinical geriatric psychopharmacology* (3rd ed., pp. 153–183). Baltimore: Williams & Wilkins.

Lararus, L. W., Newton, N., Cohler, B., Lesser, J., & Schweon, C. (1987). Frequency and presentation of depressive symptoms in patients with primary degenerative dementia. *American Journal of Psychiatry, 144*, 41–45.

Lebowitz, B. D., Pearson, J. L., & Cohen, G. D. (1998). Older Americans and their illness. In C. Salzman (Ed.), *Clinical geriatric psychopharmacology* (3rd ed., pp. 3–20). Baltimore: Williams & Wilkins.

Mulsant, B. H., Pollock, B. G., Nebes, R. D., Miller, M. D., Little, J. T., Stack, J., Houck, P. R., Bensasi, S., Mazumdar, S., & Reynolds, C. F. III. (1999). A double-bind randomized comparison of nortriptyline and paroxetine in the treatment of late-life depression: 6-week outcome. *Journal of Clinical Psychiatry, 60*(Suppl. 20), 16–20.

Nelson, J. C., Mazure, C. M., & Jatlow, P. I. (1995). Desipramine treatment of major depression in patients 75 years of age. *Journal of Clinical Psychopharmacology, 15*, 99–105.

Patel, J. E., & Salzman, C. (1998). Appendix C: Drug interactions with psychotropic medications. In C. Salzman (Ed.), *Clinical geriatric psychopharmacology* (3rd ed., pp. 553–578). Baltimore: Williams & Wilkins.

Pinsker, H., & Suljaga-Petchel, K. (1984). Use of benzodiazepines in primary-care geriatric patients. *Journal of the American Geriatric Society, 32*, 595–598.

Ray, W. A., Griffin, M. R., & Downey, M. (1989). Benzodiazepines of long- and short-elimination half-life and the risk of hip fracture. *Journal of the American Medical Association, 262*, 3303–3307.

Reifler, B. V., Teri, L., Raskind, M., Veith, R., Barnes, R., White, E., & McLean, P. (1989). Double-bind trial of imipramine in Alzheimer's disease patients with and without depression. *American Journal of Psychiatry, 146*, 45–49.

Reynolds, C. F. III, Miller, M. D., Pasternak, R. E., Frank, E., Perel, J. M., Cornes, C., Houck, P. R., Mazumdar, S., Dew, M. A., & Kupfer, D. J. (1999). Treatment of bereavement-related major depressive episodes in later life: A controlled study of acute and continuation treatment with nortriptyline and interpersonal psychotherapy. *American Journal of Psychiatry, 156*, 202–208.

Reynolds, C. F. III, Perel, J. M., Frank, E., Cornes, C., Miller, M. D., Houck, P. R., Mazumdar, S., Stack, J. A., Pollock, B. G., Dew, M. A., & Kupfer, D. J. (1999). Three-year outcomes of maintenance nortriptyline treatment in late-life depression: A study of two fixed plasma levels. *American Journal of Psychiatry, 156*, 1177–1181.

Reynolds, C. F. III, Regestein, Q., Nowell, P. D., & Neylan, T. C. (1998). Treatment of insomnia in the elderly. In C. Salzman (Ed.), *Clinical geriatric psychopharmacology* (3rd ed., pp. 395–416). Baltimore: Williams & Wilkins.

Robinson, R. G., Schultz, S. K., & Paradiso, S. (1998). Treatment of poststroke psychiatric disorders. In J. C. Nelson (Ed.), *Geriatric psychopharmacology* (pp. 161–185). New York: Marcel Dekker.

Rovner, B. W., & Katz, I. R. (1993). Psychiatric disorders in the nursing home: A selective review of studies related to clinical care. *International Journal of Geriatric Psychiatry, 8,* 75–87.

Salem-Schatz, S. R., & Fields, D. (1992). A randomized trial of a program to reduce the use of psychoactive drugs in nursing homes. *New England Journal of Medicine, 237,* 168–173.

Salzman, C. (1998). Treatment of anxiety and anxiety-related disorders. In C. Salzman (Ed.), *Clinical geriatric psychopharmacology* (3rd ed., pp. 343–368). Baltimore: Williams & Wilkins.

Salzman, C., & Sheikh, J. I. (1998). Diagnosis of anxiety and anxiety-related disorders. In C. Salzman (Ed.), *Clinical geriatric psychopharmacology* (3rd ed., pp. 333–342). Baltimore: Williams & Wilkins.

Salzman, C., Vaccaro, B., Lieff, J., & Weiner, A. (1995). Clozapine in older patients with psychosis and behavioral disruption. *American Journal of Geriatric Psychiatry, 3,* 26–33.

Salzman, C., & van der Kolk, B. (1980). Psychotropic drug prescriptions for elderly patients in a general hospital. *Journal of the American Geriatric Society, 20*(1), 18–22.

Schneider, L., & Tariot, P. (1998). Treatment of dementia. In C. Salzman (Ed.), *Clinical geriatric psychopharmacology* (3rd ed., pp. 510–542). Baltimore: Williams & Wilkins.

Schneider, L. S., Small, G. W., Hamilton, S. H., Bystritsky, A., Nemeroff, C. B., Meyers, B. S., & the Fluotetine Collaborative Study Group. (1997, Spring). Estrogen replacement and response to fluoxetine in a multicenter geriatric depression trial. *American Journal of Geriatric Psychiatry, 5,* 97–106.

Smith, B. D., & Salzman, C. (1991). Do benzodiazepines cause depression? *Hospital and Community Psychiatry, 42,* 1101–1102.

Williams-Russo, P. (1996). Barriers to diagnosis and treatment of depression in primary care settings. *American Journal of Geriatric Psychiatry, 4*(Suppl. 1), S84–S90.

INDEX

Page numbers followed by "t" indicate tables.

173